Scripture and Strategy:
The Use of the Bible
in Postmodern Church
and Mission

David J. Hesselgrave

William Carey Library

PASADENA, CALIFORNIA

Published by
William Carey Library
P.O. Box 40129
Pasadena, California 91114
(818) 798-0819

Library of Congress Cataloging-in-Publication Data

Hesselgrave, David J.
    Scripture and strategy : the use of the Bible in post-
modern church and mission / by David J. Hesselgrave.
        p.   cm.
    Includes bibliographical references.
    ISBN 0-87808-375-8 (pbk).
    1. Bible—Study and teaching.   2. Evangelistic work—
Philosophy.   3. Missions—Theory.   I. Title.
BS600.2.H454   1994   94-36869
220'.09'04—dc20   CIP

To
The Officers and Members
of the
Evangelical Missiological Society

Contents

Foreword to the Evangelical Missiological Society Series

We are navigating a "sea change" in missions today. The old paradigms, which God used so greatly in the past two centuries despite their flaws, no longer serve missions well. New ones are beginning to emerge, but not all are faithful to biblical teaching and most are untested.

This sea change is due to many factors. One is the success of the modern mission movement that has left churches in most countries around the world. Today these churches are maturing in strength and leadership, and many are involved in mission. A second factor is the changing world scene. The currents of nationalism, cultural revivalism, resurgent ethnic loyalties, urbanization, world trade and global communication networks are pulling the world in different directions. The result is growing conflicts between traditional cultures and modernity, between rival ethnic groups, between rich and poor, and between nations vying for dominance. How do we carry out our mission mandate in such turmoil? How do we free ourselves from identification with Western cultures, and manifest in our ministry the global nature of the church and mission?

In 1993 the Evangelical Missiological Society began a concerted study of the mission scene to provide guidance for evangelicals involved in missions in these times of transition. It decided to focus its conferences each year on a common theme addressing one of the major challenges facing contemporary missions, highlighting especially the theological issues involved. These challenges offer us both opportunities for greater outreach and risks of undermining the mission cause. Select papers from these conferences and from members of the association are to be published each year in a volume that focuses our attention on a critical issue in contemporary missions and provides evangelical responses to these questions. The goal is to create both awareness and discussion among missionaries and mission scholars, and to present in-depth evangelical responses to the questions.

We are privileged to present *Scripture and Strategy* by David Hesselgrave as the first volume in the series. The author has played a key role in the development of the EMS and its wide-ranging ministries. In this book he examines the place of the Bible in formulating church and mission strategy for the postmodern age which we have now entered. In doing so, he lays a foundation for discussing the various issues that will be addressed in subsequent volumes.

The second volume, to be edited by Edward Rommen and Harold Netland and published in 1995, will address the questions of religious pluralism and the uniqueness of the Gospel. The plan is to issue at least one volume each year during the remaining years of this decade, D.V. We hope that the series will help pastors, evangelists, administrators, practitioners and mission scholars see a clear way through our confusing times so that they can serve with greater faithfulness and fruitfulness. Above all we pray that the series may bring glory to our Lord and Savior, Jesus Christ, the Head of the church and the beginning and end of all missions.

Paul G. Hiebert
Chairman, Publications Committee
Evangelical Missiological Society

Foreword to
Scripture and Strategy

It must have been a sickening sight. A band of bold adventurers who had braved an unknown ocean stood on the shore of a Caribbean island and watched their ship, the *Santa Maria,* dashed to pieces on the rocks. How could anyone have let it happen? Did someone cut the anchor line? Was someone asleep on their watch? Accounts vary, but Columbus' voyage of adventure, discovery, business and missions nearly went down with that ship.

In New Testament times there were concerns that believers might drift away from their moorings and shipwreck themselves and perhaps the church as well. The writer of Hebrews, referring to salvation by faith in Christ, made known through the sure Word of God, urged his readers to "pay more careful attention to what we have heard, so that we do not drift away" (Heb. 3:1). This is the basic concern of David Hesselgrave and of this series, expecially as it relates to the missionary movement.

The biblical and theological foundations for this magnificent enterprise we call "missions" has been well laid. Writers and practitioners like Bavinck, Allen, Nevius, Kraemer, Verkuyl, Peters and Beyerhaus labored effectively to base the modern mission movement on the Word of God. The United Bible Societies and Wycliffe Bible Translators have made the Bible more than the middle name of their respective organizations. They, along with others, have worked to make the Scripture available in every language of the world. But will the churches and missions keep the Bible foundational and central to their task as the Lord grants yet more time to carry forward the missionary mandate? The thesis of *Scripture and Strategy* is that they can and must.

Michael Pocock
President, Evangelical Missiological Society

Acknowledgments

In writing this book I owe so much to so many colleagues, friends and family members that the following paragraphs could easily be extended beyond the patience required to read them. However, to overlook the contributions of at least some of these benefactors would be inexcusable. So, wtih a plea for understanding on the part of those whose names are omitted though deserving of inclusion as well as on the part of readers who will pause to read these lines, I will proceed.

First of all, I express my appreciation to faithful colleagues at home and abroad whose faithfulness to Christ, his Word and his cause have both inspired and informed this book. The list is long, but all whose works and writings are highlighted in the following chapters would certainly be included. In addition, Carl Henry, William Larkin, Paul Hiebert, Timothy Warner, John Piper and Ralph Winter made themselves available to review chapters focusing on their respective and related writings. In several sections of this book I have leaned rather heavily on certain writings of David Wells and Walter Kaiser. They reviewed this entire manuscript and made valuable suggestions. A number of others have kindly responded to my request for their insights and evaluations. My secretary in the School of World Mission and Evangelism at Trinity Evangelical Divinity

School, Linda Walters, helped out at critical junctures. I am greatly indebted to them all.

Since this book is the first in a series being projected by the Evangelical Missiological Society, it is appropriate that I express gratitude to the entire membership both for the privilege of serving them as executive director and the opportunity to contribute this first volume in the series. I am especially grateful to the former EMS president, Paul Beals, the current president, Michael Pocock, the publications chairman, Paul Hiebert, and the members of the executive and publications committees for all they have done to make this publication possible.

As always, members of my immediate and extended families deserve mention. My wife Gertrude undertook duties that I should rightly share and thus made this writing possible. My son, Ronald Paul, proofread the manuscript. My son-in-law Martin Kroeker put it on Microsoft Word. And my nephew, Ric DuBois, designed the cover.

Finally, I want to recognize the special contributions of David Shaver, Jone Bosch, Ralph Winter and all who are in any way connected with William Carey Library. For many years now all of us who are concerned with Great Commission mission have been the beneficiaries of their sacrificial service in publishing and distributing missionary literature. This book, being the first in the EMS series, has required special attention and effort. They are to be commended for the way in which they have responded. I offer them my special thanks.

My readers will be aware of the fact that this book is in some ways unique. But it is not unique in that it has its limitations and shortcomings. Insofar as these accrue to human disabilities of one sort or another, I acknowledge them as my own. My solace is that there is one Book that rises above the weaknesses of any of its human authors, and this book is designed to direct its readers to *that* Book and its Divine Author. Of several excellent modern translations of the Bible, I have elected to quote most often from the New American Standard Bible except in those cases where another translation is indicated. Therefore I express my thanks to The Lockman Foundation and the NASB translators.

David J. Hesselgrave
Deerfield, Illinois

Part I

Introduction

1

Back to the Future

Have you noticed? A quiet revolution is going on. Amidst all the noisy revolutions—made noisy by detonations, demonstrations, and demagoguery—there is one that has largely escaped notice. It is occurring in the church and its missions. For that reason as well as others, it is accompanied by little fanfare and has captured minimal press. But it is happening. And it is hopeful. Hopeful for the church. Hopeful for the mission. Hopeful for the world.

This book has to do with that quiet revolution, with the strategy that characterizes it, and with Christian leaders who have contributed to it. To understand the potential of this hopeful aspect of contemporary Christian witness and ministry it would be helpful to trace some contours of the emerging world.

A Look Around:
The Postmodern World

Our part of the world at least has been characterized as post-Christian for some time now. We can quarrel with the term if we want, but the Western world is post-Christian in the sense that governmental and educational institutions not only refuse to take Christian values for granted, they seldom take them into account. Also in the sense that, while the a significant part of the larger society tenaciously clings to "inalienable rights," it implacably disregards the Creator apart from whom those rights are neither self-evident nor sustainable.

Now the Western world is being characterized as postmodern as well. There is less agreement on what it means to be postmodern, but it is apparent that there is a widespread disenchantment with the premises, promises and productions of the modern era. The optimism that accrued to the dawning of the Enlightenment and the rise of modern science has somehow dissipated in the smoke of Hiroshima and Nagasaki and strife in the streets of Los Angeles and Sarajevo. For over a hundred years would-be Christians as well as confessed skeptics have brought Scripture and Christian faith to the bar of human reason. During the years that Scripture has been on trial, people have placed implicit faith in science—secure in the belief that, given more time, science would answer our questions and solve our problems. The key phrase here is "given more time." But already time is running out. And people are looking elsewhere. They probe the depths of the human spirit. They look to the stars. They investigate Eastern mysticism. What they find is not objective truth but intuition, feeling and experience. Psychologies, philosophies, religions abound, but none provides *the* truth, only "truth for me" or you or someone else. In all, most people remain hopeful, not because the facts of contemporary life warrant optimism but because optimism is the last bastion of sanity and self-preservation.

G. Edward Veith, Jr., indicates that postmodern humanity creates not only its own "truth"; it also exalts power. So society fragments into competing power groups each exerting a will to power that expresses itself in practical anarchy and lawlessness. Finally, postmodern humanity searches for law and order at any price. The political outcome is fascism (Veith 1994).

A variety of terms and characterizations, then, have been used to characterize the postmodern world, depending upon whether one's perspective is political, moral, social, philosophical, or religious. Our present perspective is philosophical and religious. Our concern is for the discovery and dissemination of the revealed truth of God in the face of subjectivism, relativism, and religious pluralism. For postmodern men and women, any truth but their own "truth" is in short supply and absolute truth is undiscoverable. Religion used to provide it for many, but, now that adherents of so many religions surround us, postmoderns are quite assured that all have *some* truth but none has *the* truth.

But what about the non-Western world? Perhaps hope for the future lies somewhere in Asia or Africa or Latin America or the Middle East or the Island World? Perhaps so, but it seems less likely with every passing day, especially when we view the situation rationally rather than romantically. The noble savage of yesterday's pseudo-anthropology now appears to have been a product of Western myth-making. Upon careful examination, the ancient religions of the East hold little hope for life in this world and mostly mystification with respect to any future one.

A quarter century ago in Nigeria, a British expert on African affairs told us that there is no way Africa can leapfrog into the modern world without decades of bitterness and bloodshed. We now know he was right. At the moment, post-apartheid South Africa is one of the more hopeful nations and their chief economic hope lies in the manufacturing of high-tech military equipment!

Perhaps nothing is more indicative of dramatic change in the non-Western world than a pervasive disenchantment with the West itself—with its types of democracy, its morals, its values, and even its peoples—though there remains a desire for freedom and technology. In fact, in almost every nation there is a pronounced tendency to return to centuries-old folkways, traditions, religions and loyalties. It is not unlikely that those nations that have only recently modernized will also become postmodern, and that others will become "postmodern" without ever becoming really "modern"!

A Look Back:
The World of the Bible

It is common to think of the biblical world faced by the prophets and the apostles as a world apart. But that perception is in great measure molded by imagination. Some imagine it to have been a naive world in which everyone was ready to believe almost any superstition or fairy tale. Actually, it was a world with which contemporary students of philosophy begin their studies and then discover whether or not they are good enough to continue. Some view the biblical world as a world devoid of all science and technology whereas the people of that world actually produced architectural marvels that baffle engineers to this very day. Some think of the world of the Bible as so culturally different that moderns cannot be expected to understand it, or learn anything from it if they do. Actually it is our modern Western, particularly American, culture that is so culturally distant from both the ancient world and the rest of our contemporary world that others have a difficult time understanding us and learning much of lasting value if they do.

Nowadays perceptions are in flux. In the modern era Western culture was largely sealed off from other cultures except as it sent its explorers and entrepreneurs to their shores. Now uncounted millions of erstwhile foreigners come to us with their languages, folkways and alliances. More than that, they insist upon their right to maintain their own cultural identity. The West itself has become multicultural.

More important from our perspective is the fact that, in the modern era, the West was largely sealed off from other religions except as our missionaries encountered and reported them. As we have indicated, that too has changed. In 1993 Chicago groups representing over a dozen religions hosted a Parliament of the World's Religions. Some 7,000 guests of a wide variety of religious persuasions ranging from the historic faiths to witchcraft and modern cults attended. As this is being written, leaders of a Chicago-area African cult are demanding that 200 sacrificial animals and birds seized by Chicago authorities be returned so that worship rituals can continue.

Concerning religious pluralism David Wells writes,

> But while religious pluralism may be a novel experience for us, it is putting us in touch with the world that surrounded the biblical authors probably more directly than others. The pluralism and paganism of Our Time were the common experience of the prophets and apostles. In Mesopotamia, there were thousands of gods and goddesses, many of which were known to the Israelites—indeed, sometimes known too well. In Christ's time, there were hundreds of sects of one kind or another along the Mediterranean rim. Moreover, there was the official Roman religion that blended politics and religion through a deification of the Caesars, in due course becoming a formidable enemy of the Christian faith. And there was Greek philosophy as well, much of it also functioning as a set of competing religions. Pluralism was the stuff of everyday life in biblical times. (Wells 1992: 263).

Yes, indeed it *was* the "stuff" of biblical times. It is the "stuff" of today. And, increasingly, it promises to be the "stuff" of tomorrow.

A Look Ahead:
The Postmodern World of Tomorrow

Whereas we tend to rush into the future without looking back, ancestor-oriented peoples in general, and tribals in particular, "back into the future." For them, the ancestors not only supply the story of the past; they also supply wisdom and direction for the future. The ancestors are always celebrated and often consulted. No crisis is faced, no decision made, without calling upon those to whom the tribe, clan or family owe their very existence. Eyes and ears are ever trained on those revered progenitors to whom the people of today themselves will be joined in the near future. Missionaries can attest to the fact that, viewed in this way, the past becomes a major obstacle to decision-making and even to planning.

But if others err in learning too much from those who preceded them and in leaning on them too much, we err in learning too little. The Bible has much to say about remembering the past. And the biblical term (*anamnēsis* in New Testament Greek) "carries the important dynamic meaning of a recalling from the past into the present of an action which lies buried in history, in such a way that the result of past action is made potentially present" (Martin 1959: 153). It was just that kind of "recalling from the past" that lent a quiet but contagious confidence to the ministry of the prophets and apostles. To quote Wells again,

> The prophets of the Old Testament and the apostles of the New . . . take the modern breath away, for they had a certainty about the existence, character, and purposes of God—a certainty about his truth—that seems to have faded in the bright light of the modern world. They were convinced that God's revelation, of which they were vehicles and custodians, was true. True in an absolute sense. It was not merely true *to them;* it was not merely true *in their time;* it was not true *approximately.* What God had given was true universally, absolutely, and enduringly (Wells 1992: 259-60).

It is just that kind of remembering and reassurance that both the church and the world needs today, and will need increasingly in the future. Lesslie Newbigin writes of a "plausibility structure" that more and more has come to characterize our world—a mindset which is unthinkingly suspicious of truth claims such as those inherent in the Christian gospel. From a theological position quite distinct from that of David Wells, he nevertheless insists that what is needed is a new *arche* or starting-point for thought. And that starting-point must be God's revelation of his being and purpose in Scripture (Newbigin 1991: 28).

The underlying thesis of this book is that Holy Scripture itself must occupy a central place in the future strategy of the churches and their missions. To reinforce that thesis we will look at the testimony of Scripture Author/authors; we will review in broad outline some of the ways in which representatives of church and mission have used (and abused) Scripture in modern times; and we will take special notice of the ministries of some of our colleagues who in my view demonstrate that, rightly viewed and used, the Bible itself possesses the highest potential for impacting a postmodern world for Christ.

This close associaton of Scripture and strategy requires some explanation. The word "strategy," of course, comes from Greek and is a military term (though *strategos* is primarily used of magistrates in the New Testament). It has to do with the art and science of employing resources in such a way as to secure the objectives of an army—by analysis, planning, recruitment, deployment, and so forth.

The term is quite often used in church and mission circles, though the less demanding term "method" is more widely used. "Method" (*meta*, "after" plus *hodos*, "way" or "road") is a regularized way of going about a task; a procedure followed in order to achieve a certain end. Our thesis, then, is that the Old and New Testament Scriptures constitute more than the substance of God's purpose, plan and pronouncements vis-a-vis our world; they also constitute an essential part of his strategy for announcing and achieving his purpose. At the procedural level we would maintain that the Bible contains more than a divine message, it constitutes a divine method of delivering that message.

If I understand him correctly, John Stott has something similar in mind when he writes:

> the Bible does not just *contain* the gospel; it *is* the gospel. Through the Bible God is himself actually evangelizing, that is, communicating the good news to the world. You will recall Paul's statement about Genesis 12:3 that 'the scripture . . . preached the gospel beforehand to Abraham' (Gal. 3:8; RSV). All Scripture preaches the gospel; God evangelizes through it (Stott 1992: A6; emphasis his).

The upshot is that, while citizens of the world have looked for hope in all the wrong places, it is possible that many of God's saints who minister to them have been looking for ministry helps in all the wrong places. Augustine was right when he insisted that both qualitively and quantitatively more of essential truth is to be found in Scripture than in all the learning of the world. We need to look once again to the prophets and apostles, and to our Lord himself. We need to review the record of the fathers and the reformers. Concerning Luther and the Bible, the nineteenth-century historian Merle D'Aubigné wrote:

> Thus, as the doctrine of the Bible had impelled Luther's contemporaries toward Jesus Christ, their love for Jesus Christ, in its turn, impelled them toward the Bible. It was not, as some in our days have supposed, from a philosophical necessity, or from doubt, or a spirit of inquiry that they reverted to Scripture, it was because they found there the word of Him they loved. "You have preached Christ," said they to the Reformer, "let us now hear him himself." And they

caught at the sheets given to the world, as a letter coming from heaven (D'Aubigné 1840: 3. 104).

We also need to remember the impact of the Old Testament (primarily in the form of the Septuagint Greek translation!) on the early church and its first-century world as well as the influence of the Authorized Version upon the entire English-speaking world in recent centuries. And we should review the place of the Bible in evangelism and mission as traced by A. M. Chirgwin in *The Bible in World Evangelism* (1954), Arthur P. Johnston in *World Evangelism and the Word of God* (1974), a special issue of *The International Review of Mission* (1981, No. 279) and elsewhere.

Most of the foregoing must of necessity remain outside of our purview here, but we will highlight the approaches of some missionaries and evangelists, and pastors and theologians of recent times. Through their ministries we will see again that which has been evident throughout the longer history of the people of God. Namely, that progress seems always to be linked with complete confidence in, and careful examination and utilization of, the revealed Word of God.

Several caveats are in order before we proceed. First, the task to which we have set ourselves is not to reinforce a simplistic understanding and use of the Bible on the one hand, nor is it to denigrate the importance of understandings that accrue to general revelation and the so-called secular sciences on the other. As for the former extreme, the chapters that follow should provide ample evidence that I do not subscribe to it. As for the latter notion, even a cursory examination of my published works will show that I myself have made extended use of the findings of the social sciences.

Second, the Christian leaders whose work is highlighted here are by no means alone in taking the path they have taken and pointing a way for the future. There are many others, some of whom are mentioned in these pages and many of whom, of necessity, are omitted. Of those merely mentioned and all who are omitted, I ask for undestanding. I have tried to select some who are older, some who are younger; some of my own ecclesiastical tradition, some of others; some with whom I am personally acquainted, some whom I have never met. All of them have kept church and mission together. All of them have had an unusual impact upon churches and missions worldwide. All of them have blessed and informed my own life and ministry. All of them will, I believe, bless and inform the ministry of the reader.

Third, readers are encouraged to continue the investigation that is barely begun here. My colleagues in and out of the Evangelical Missiological Society have been so kind as to suggest a host of relevant topics that time and space do not allow me to deal with in a volume of this size. In each chapter I have attempted to fill in the main contours of the historical context to which God has called us to respond. Doing this in bold strokes is somewhat risky and invites more study. Further investigation into what I have called the "quiet revolution" would be welcome. Numerous productions and programs deserve careful attention that cannot be given here: Bruce Wilkinson's "Walk Thru the Bible Ministries"; Terry Hall's *Bible Panorama, Old Testament Express,* and *New Testament Express* (Victor); *The Divine Drama* produced by Harry Wendt of Crossways International; the Baptist Sunday School Board's *Step by Step Through the Old Testament* and *Step by Step Through the New Testament;* and still others.

Fourth, the author recognizes that biblical revelation takes forms other than that of the printed page. Though the emphasis here is on the Bible as the Book of God, its words and message can be transmitted in an oral tradition, through pictures, in drama and other ways.

FIFTH, DEPENDING UPON A VARIETY OF FACTORS, READERS WILL FIND CERTAIN OF THE FOLLOWING CHAPTERS MORE SUITED TO THEIR INTERESTS AND BACKGROUND THAN OTHERS. FOR EXAMPLE, THE NEXT CHAPTER IN PART II HIGH-

LIGHTS VARIOUS VIEWS OF BIBLICAL AUTHORITY
AND CARL F. H. HENRY'S DEFENSE OF VERBAL-
PLENARY INSPIRATION. IT IS AN EXTREMELY IM-
PORTANT CHAPTER AND LOGICALLY IT TAKES
PRECEDENCE OVER THE OTHERS. BUT FOR SOME IT
WILL BE RATHER PONDEROUS AND EVEN IN-
TIMIDATING IN SPITE OF OUR BEST EFFORT TO
MAKE IT OTHERWISE. NO MATTER. THE READER
SHOULD LOOK AHEAD TO A CHAPTER THAT MATCH-
ES HIS OR HER INTERESTS AND INVOLVEMENT. THE
LOGIC THAT ORDERS THE SEQUENCE FOLLOWED
HERE CAN BE MADE A MATTER OF LATER CONCERN.

Part II

The Place of the Bible
In Christian Thought

2

Carl F. H. Henry: Recovering Biblical Authority

"By what authority?" Voiced or unvoiced, that basic question faces the churches and their missions today. Evangelists, pastors, teachers, and counselors face it in Western cultures that have been shorn of absolutes. Expatriate missionaries and Third World nationals face it in non-Western cultures still addicted to false gods and gurus.

It is not a new question. Moses faced it (Ex. 5:1-2). Elijah faced it (1 Kgs. 18:21). Paul faced it (Acts 17:18). Our Lord himself faced it (Matt. 21:23). The Fathers and Reformers faced it. A century ago our forebears faced it. And now we face it in a world increasingly characterized by a cacophony of competing truth claims.

"By what authority?" The question has been answered by Christians in a variety of ways. Some have appealed to the authority of the church. Others to tradition. Still others to reason. In contemporary missions it has become popular to appeal to personal experience ("It worked for me"); to open confrontation with evil powers ("power encounter"); and to identification with the felt needs of people ("They will know by our love").

Depending upon context and meaning, all of these and still other answers have some utility. But the univocal and unequivocal answer of the patriarchs and prophets, evangelists and apostles, fathers and reformers, and, most importantly, Christ himself to the question of authority has been "Thus saith the Lord"/"It is written." If, as Karl Barth is reported to have affirmed on one occasion, the profundity of the biblical gospel is expressible in the simple words "Jesus loves me, this I know," the essence of a biblical apologetic can be expressed as "For the Bible tells me so." None of us understands it completely or perfectly; none of us communicates it fully or adequately; but as the divine Author/human authors originally gave it, Scripture itself is complete, perfect and adequate.

As for our part, either we proclaim the divine, objective, absolute revelation from the God of the universe or we proffer the human, subjective, tentative opinion of this or that fallen, erring worldling. The world of the future will not lack for the latter. To the degree that there is to be a death-dealing spiritual famine, it will be a famine of truth, a hungering for the Word of God. In one of its simplest formulations, therefore, the task of churches and their missions is to see that such a famine does not occur.

Authority and the World's Religious Traditions and Sacred Books

In the past, discussions on biblical authority have not usually begun with a consideration of Hinduism and the Vedas, Buddhism and the Tripitaka, Islam and the Qu'ran, and so on. But that is the logical place to start. And it will be the strategic place to start in tomorrow's world. Increasingly, behind questions having to do with *biblical* authority will lurk the specter of competing authorities inherent in the sacred books of the non-Christian religious traditions. This will be so in the West as it has always been so in the East.

Concerning this, Eric J. Sharpe writes,

> since virtually all scripture is understood in revelatory terms . . . there must be some prior understanding of Hindu, Jewish, Christian, Muslim and other doctrines of God and doctrines of revelation (Sharpe 1971: 64-65).

This is true even in the case of religions that are not ordinarily classified as "revealed religions."

The first chapter of Romans makes it clear that God has made certain truths about his person and nature clear by the things that he has made (Rom. 1:20). Indeed, there is a "true light which, coming into the world, enlightens every man" (John 1:9). "Natural" or "general" revelation, therefore, is affirmed by Scripture. Early on, however, most people preferred human speculation to divine revelation and devoted themselves to creature-like gods of their own making (Rom. 1:21-23). They also made up stories about these gods and attributed certain utterances to them and their representatives. Elsewhere I have elaborated a typology of the various scriptures that contain these stories and utterances (Hesselgrave and Rommen 1989: 128-43). They are of three main types. The Old and New Testament Scriptures are very different and constitute a fourth type.

1) Some scriptures are essentially *mythological*. I use the word "mythological" here to refer to the records of extraordinary narratives and utterances held to convey basic information about god(s) and other supernatural beings, and the world and humankind, which bind a people together in a common origin, loyalty and destiny. Most tribal societies have an oral myth of this kind which can be treated very much as if it were available in written form.

Classic examples of scriptures of this type are the Kojiki, Nihongi and Engishiki of the Shinto religion. Though these books contain some history, it is almost impossible to determine where myth leaves off and history begins, and in any case, the distinction is not important to Shintoists. Mythological scriptures are not authoritative because they provide accurate history, genuine, authentic and (objectively) true, and therefore little attention is given to matters having to do with authorship and textual variants. Rather, the authority of such scriptures rests in the fact that, for the people (race, nation, tribe, clan, community) who hold to them, they provide a basis for the origin and destiny, beliefs and values, rituals and institutions that provide meaning to life and hold the people together as a people. Adherents—especially their leaders—decide what is myth and what is history, and how the text is to be understood and used, depending on human reason and purpose.

2) The *reports, teachings and instructions of certain uniquely inspired and enlightened men* constitute another type of scripture. Among the world's sacred books the Hindu Vedas, the Tao-Teh-Ching of Taoism and the Buddhist Tripitaka are of this type. Once again, the authority of these scriptures does not reside in historicity or even authenticity. They are reputed to be the products of men who experienced ultimate understanding and emancipation (the early *rishis* or wise men of India, Lao-tze, Gautama Buddha), but whether or not those men actually authored them is not a matter of great consequence. Their importance lies in the fact that they possess the potential for occasioning the same or similar experiences in those who believe and practice them as were experienced by those who authored the initial reports. If the reputed authors were not the actual authors (as is often the case), no matter. If they are true, they are not made true because this or that teacher spoke or wrote them, and if they are not true, it makes no difference who spoke or authored them. Their truth and authority reside in their potential for guiding adepts into the en-

lightenment experience. For those thus aided, they obviously are authoritative. For others—what difference do they make? Authority is in the experience, not in the text.

3) *Divine writings* constitute a third type of scripture. Though certain sects of both the Eastern and Western worlds such as Mormonism stake claim to the possession of scriptures of this type, the classic example is, of course, the Qu'ran.

Though Muhammad is said to have had various supernatural visions and to have been Allah's spokesman, the Qu'ran itself is held by Muslims to be something totally other than a record of the visions and inspiration of the prophet. The Qu'ran is reputed to be an exact replica of the "Mother of the Book" in heaven. Its words are said to have been dictated to Muhammad and recorded by him quite apart from any literary talent or extraordinary insight that he himself might have possessed. The Qu'ran, therefore, is held to be Allah's word and will and in that claim rests its authority.

Interestingly, as in the cases of the "myth" and "reports" varieties of scripture, traditional Muslim scholarship eschews textual studies of the kind we have associated with even lower criticism. No matter that Muhammad inscribed the text on everything from stones to bones. No matter that competing texts were suppressed and destroyed, especially under Uthman. No matter that to imprison the Qu'ran in the Arabic language means that it cannot be translated and results in a profound provincialism. By definition, to be a Muslim means to surrender. And one of the things that must be surrendered in these matters is one's reason. The authority of the Qu'ran is blind authority.

4) *It is of the utmost importance that we understand and communicate the fact that the Old and New Testament Scriptures are distinct from any of the foregoing revelational types (and especially types one and two above), not alone in its message but also its authority. The holy men of the Bible spoke as they were moved by the Holy Spirit (2 Pet. 1:21). The Bible was given by inspiration of God; it was "God-breathed" (2 Tim. 3:16-17). More on this later. At any rate, Christian apol-*

ogists and theologians often speak of "dual authorship" and sometimes refer to the biblical "Author/authors." In so doing they are not referring to some new game! They mean that in biblical revelation the Triune God used human authors (along with their unique experiences, abilities and personalities) in such a way as to provide bibical books that are indeed the words of patriarch, prophet and apostle but also the words of God.

B. B. Warfield, Carl F. H. Henry, Gordon H. Clark, E. J. Young, Gleason Archer, Cornelius Van Til, John F. Walvoord, Kenneth S. Kantzer and numerous others have devoted considerable effort to show that biblical revelation is not mythological but historical; not just or primarily personal and subjective but propositional and objective; not just instrumental and potentially effective but cognitively true and continuously active; and not the result of mechanical dictation but nevertheless infallible and free from internal contradiction and error. This is in agreement with the conclusions of the Fathers and the Reformers. Most importantly, it is in agreement with New Testament writers and Christ himself, all of whom "habitually appeal to the Old Testament text as to God himself speaking" (Warfield as quoted in Wells 1990: 162).

Authority, the Bible and the Church

The Enlightenment and the emergence of the so-called Scientific Age occasioned an unprecedented challenge to the authority of the Bible. Modern humanity became obsessed with their ability to explain on natural grounds more and more of that part of knowledge that had been consigned to the Almighty. Only what could be proved rationally and scientifically could be accepted intellectually. The scientific method became the door to knowledge and human reason the final arbiter. The mood was optimistic. What remained in doubt today would be proved or disproved tomorrow.

Protestant scholars of the late nineteenth and early twentieth centuries especially took another look at the biblical text, sometimes not so much to learn from it as to pass judgment upon it. The studies to which I am referring were not undertaken in order to discover manuscript evidence, or to decide upon the most faithful rendering of the text, or to deliberate on other matters that constitute the subject matter of what is often referred to as *lower criticism*. Rather, they were *higher critical* studies which passed judgment upon the text, determining what could be accepted and on what basis and in what sense.

Literary- and historical-critical methods militated against a trustworthy Bible. Relying on the history of literary genres, form criticism assumed that much of Scripture was passed down from generation to generation orally and was shaped by these successive communities. Redaction criticism alleged that significant portions of Scripture represent the work of later editors rather than of the authors to whom they are assigned. Some critics took it upon themselves to date biblical books on the basis of correlation with the events and understandings of certain peoples and times. Others rejected the factualness of biblical miracles, arguing that, because the recording of them reflected the pre-scientific worldview of biblical times, moderns could not be expected to accept supernatural explanations such as these. And so on.

Higher critical approaches to the Bible have had a profound impact upon the thinking and doings of the twentieth-century church in the West and also in the East. Early in this century, for example, Harry Emerson Fosdick wrote a book entitled *The Modern Use of the Bible* (1924) in which he attempted to demonstrate that the Bible has utility and value despite the fact that moderns cannot be expected to accept it at face value.

At a different level neo-Protestant theologians did something similar. Karl Barth attempted to rescue biblical authority by asserting that the real content of the Bible is not conceptual and does not yield general truth. What is conceptual is the human part and only "points to" the Word of God which is always personal. The Bible is authoritative in the sense that in it resides the potential for becoming the Word of God to the person who reads it.

Rudolph Bultmann believed that a book of stories about iron floating, thousands fed with a boy's lunch, the blind made to see, to say nothing of the dead coming back to life, possessed little credibility in a scientific age. The Bible, therefore, needs to be "demythologized." When it is, men and women are somehow enabled to encounter the "Christ of Scripture" and, in him, the divine reality and love that demand an inner decision. Irrespective of its mythological content, he held that the Scripture is nevertheless authoritative in this sense.

Paul Tillich basically agreed with Bultmann but took exception to the idea of "demythologizing." He agreed that the Bible is essentially mythological but insisted that its myths are rich in symbols that "point to something outside of themselves." Creation, the Kingdom, and Christ as the Son of God may have little to do with history as such. As symbols, however, they express deep and abiding truths for all who are concerned about the ultimate. Tillich's use of the Bible, therefore, involved "deliteralizing biblical myths" and exposing their symbolic significance.

Still others (e.g., Krister Stendahl and Paul Knitter) have held that the significance and authority of the Bible is to be found in what it means to the reader or hearer. The assertions of the apostles—for example, Peter's affirmation that Jesus is the Christ, the Son of the living God—may have no more objective meaning than when a man says his wife is the most "beautiful woman in the world." Nevertheless, the statements of Peter and the other apostles can stimulate faith and in that sense they are authoritative.

Now all of these and many others who take the same or similar positions may be sincere in their attempt to rescue *some kind of authority* for the Bible. But in the process they actually substitute one or another kind of human authority for divine authority. More than that, it can now be seen that, in effect, they have assigned the Old and New Testament Scriptures to those same or similar categories to which Shintoists consign the Kojiki, Buddhists consign the Tripitaka, Hindus consign the Vedas, and Taoists consign the Tao-Teh-Ching! When that is done, proclamation is reduced to the status of proposal. "Thus saith the Lord!" is of little or no more significance than "Thus spoke Zarathustra" or "The Enlightened One said."

Of course, the solution does not lie in some dictation theory that assigns the Bible to a "divine writing" status similar to that ascribed to the Qu'ran or the Book of Mormon. That would not only be to force the Bible into an ossified and untranslatable form, it would fly in the face of fact and the testimony of Scripture to itself.

Carl F. H. Henry on the Authority and Inspiration of the Bible

Arguably one of the most prolific, widely read, and frequently quoted defenders of biblical authority is Carl F. H. Henry. Professor of Systematic Theology at Fuller and then Trinity, Founding Editor of *Christianity Today,* Lecturer-at-Large for World Vision International and Prison Fellowship, author of thirty-six books and contributor to many more, Henry has been in the forefront of what Harold Lindsell termed the "battle for the Bible" for well over a generation.

Of the various authors and practitioners from whom we will draw insights and inspiration in this volume, in no other case will space constraints require a greater injustice. By far the most exhaustive and creative of Henry's writings on the authority of Scripture is that found in Volume IV of his monumental six-volume *God, Revelation and Authority* (Henry 1976-84). Here we can do no more than review the outline and thrust of his introduction to the subject entitled "The Authority and Inspiration of the Bible"—the very first article in *The Expositor's Bible Commentary* (Henry in Gaebelein, gen. ed., vol. I: 3-35). Though written some fifteen years ago, the tempered faith and trenchant reasoning of that monograph might well serve church and mission people well for many years to come. Having "set the stage" upon which church and mission people will be called upon to validate their authority, in what follows my aim is to be as faithful to Henry's presentation as possible within the brief scope allowable here. (All references are to pages in the aforementioned monograph.)

I. Introduction

The Bible is the sacred Christian book. The fate of Christianity turns on "its supernatural origin, the factuality of its redemptive history, and the validity of its teaching" (p. 3). With that profound and provocative assertion, Henry begins his case. The frequent use of the singular to refer to the Bible connotes the Christian conviction that the sixty-six books of the Old and New Testament constitute one unified utterance from God—not merely an anthology of assorted writings but one comprehensive and unified divine utterance. As such it is distinct from the sacred books of Hinduism, Buddhism, Confucianism, Zoroastrianism and other religions. The living God appears as the "speaking God" only in Judaism, Christianity and Islam among the great religions, and the Qu'ran as the product of one man, Muhammad, borrows extensively from the Bible, and makes claims that the New Testament reserves for Christ as the personal *Logos* of God.

II. The Authority of the Bible

"The first fact to be affirmed about the Bible is its divine authority" (p. 4).

A. God's Word as Rationally Intelligible

God articulates his revelation in intelligible propositions, in rational communication. Secular religious philosophers of the more distant past jeopardized their case when
they ignored intelligible divine self-disclosure. Some neo-
Protestant theologians of the more recent past have erred in
emphasizing only God's self-disclosure and have missed the
significance of revelation as a mental act. Logical positivism
stands self-discredited because its own credo (only on the basis
of scientific empiricism can statements be considered meaningful or unmeaningful) could not stand that test of ver-
ifiability. The failure of these alternatives as well as the witness
of Scripture itself reinforce (and account for revived interest in)
the rational-verbal character of divine disclosure.

B. God's Word as Dynamically Vital

There is no authority other than that established by God
(Rom. 13:1). The biblical emphasis on God's Word as a powerful Word is evident from creation in Genesis to judgment in
Revelation. God's Word shares his own attributes—living, active, powerful, and penetrating. Does the Protestant principle of
sola scriptura absolutize or "divinize" what is really relative?
No. Just the reverse. On the other hand, every attack upon
Scripture, every exotic theological notion that undermines its
authority, substitutes the relative authority of humans for the
absolute authority of the God who speaks in Scripture and
therefore works against spirit and life rather than fostering
them. It is through the Word of God reliably conveyed in
Scripture that God instructed, warned and judged Israel and
that God in Christ governs his church. The Bible is not a me-
morialized divine Word of the past that is no longer the Word
of God for us. It is the living Word of God present in the form
and content of Scripture through which the Spirit addresses us
and imparts life to us today.

C. God's Word as Deliberately Written

"That the authoritative Word of God has the written form of Scripture is not a decision left to the prophets or apostles, but one inherent in God's intention for special revelation from the very first" (p. 11). There is no way to another Word, no basis of appeal to any other authority, no private revelation which will allow us to "pick and choose," no tradition or consensus that equips us to discern its "real sense" (as though it were obscure) or supplement Scripture (as though it were insufficient and incomplete!). It is not dead because it is written! Why should the written Word be a diminution of the oral prophetic-apostolic proclamation? "The canonical Scriptures are . . . God's providential gift to the church, preserving the community of faith from vulnerability to legend, superstition, unfounded tradition, corruptive invention, and much else" (p. 12). Even our Lord Jesus thwarted the text-twisting and deceptive Satan, not by appealing to some authority that transcends Scripture, but by facing him with the unchangeable written Word of God (Matt. 4:7, 10).

III. The Inspiration of the Bible

"If divine authority is the first feature predicated of the Bible, what is next most prominently affirmed is its divine inspiration" (p. 13). God "breathed out" what the sacred writers convey. We might use the word *expiration* or the word *spiration*, but these words also are problematical.

> The emphasis falls on divine initiative and impartation rather than on human creativity; Scripture owes its origin and nature to what God breathed out. In short, the Bible's life-breath as a literary deposit is divine (p. 13).

A. Does God Speak to Hunanity?

God speaks as well as acts. He not only addresses humankind universally through nature, history, and the reason and conscience of humans. He does so articulately to chosen persons in a special way. Over and over we read, "The word of the Lord came to . . . " (Jer. 1:1,2; Hos. 1:1; Mic. 1:1). This is not figurative. Nor is it the confessional statements of the historic churches. At the same time, it is not to be understood as meaning that God literally talked by forming words and using vocal chords since God is Spirit. He did not dictate the Bible. Nevertheless, it does not do justice to the claims of the biblical authors (cf. 1 Thess. 2:13) to conclude that inspiration has to do with the truths or the message or the ideas but not the words of Scripture. "Whatever must be said for dreams, visions, and the like, the prophets themselves, and the apostle Paul likewise, find in the intelligibly communicated Word of God the fixed center of revelation" (p. 19). Henry quotes Geoffrey Bromiley at this point:

> The main point about verbal inspiration is not that the words are inspired rather than their content, but that there is no such thing without the other. . . . The content is not to be had without this form (p. 20).

B. *The Witness of the Bible Itself to Divine Inspiration*

The doctrine of biblical inspiration is under attack not only by those who reject the supernatural but by theists who insist that it inadequately reflects the biblical data. The literary-historical method per se did not require a low view of biblical authority and inspiration, but its subordination to pantheism and developmentalism has had that result. The emphasis on a community-shaped oral tradition in form criticism leaves little room for the evangelical view of inspiration. Incisive passages such as 2 Timothy 3:16 and 1 Peter 1:21 are said to mirror the devout sentiment of apostolic times, but no more than this.

But history says something very contrary to these approaches. The New Testament view has deep roots in the Old Testament. Not only do the prophets often preface their written proclamation with *debar yahweh* ("the word of the Lord") but this phrase is often used as a cover phrase for the collections of their communications in book form (cf. Hos. l:1, Joel 1:1, Mic. 1:1, Jer. 1:1). Some critics regard this as a "petrifying of the dynamic nature of the term." Others attribute this formula to the hand of a later redactor. Still others say that the failure of certain prophets to use this formula implies that not all prophets shared the *debar yahweh* view. But none of these positions will stand up under close scrutiny of the prophets.

Furthermore, the Old Testament claim to written revelation does not begin with the prophets. The claim begins with the Mosaic writings with no intimation that their dynamic force is lessened by their inscripturation (cf. Exod. 31:18; Deut. 4:13, 5:22, 9:10, 10:2, 4).

Finally, "The honor in which Jesus of Nazareth held the Old Testament at once attests the intention of the prophets and presages the attitude of the apostles toward Scripture [as possessing normative authority in its entirety]" (p. 22).

C. Modern Redefinitions of Inspiration

Prior to World War I anti-intellectualist emphasis in religion focused on the limitations of human reason and the non-theoretical nature of religious experience. Subsequently the emphasis has been on divine self-disclosure as understood in dialectical or existential terms. But the biblical doctrine of inspiration is part of a larger constellation of convictions. Though the term *propositional revelation* may seem inappropriate because the Bible includes various literary forms (poetry, parable, prophecy, etc.) and revelational mediums (dreams, visions, theophanies, etc.), nevertheless it conveys the fundamental notion that the Bible contains a body of divinely revealed objective truth.

The denial that divine revelation embraces the communication of revealed information about God and his purposes for man and the world has as its consequence the reduction of theology from a science of the transcendent God to a game of dart-throwing at a nebulous infinity (p. 23).

The neo-Protestant move away from divine self-disclosure as having to do, not with intelligible truth, but with vague and broad human experience stems from the impetus provided by Schleiermacher. According to the *Heilsgeschichte* theory, revelation is found in God's special acts in history, and the significance of the Bible is that it is a record provided and interpreted by those who were contemporaneous with the events. According to the dialectical view developed by Barth and popularized by Brunner, revelation is personal and non-propositional and the importance of the Bible is that it "witnesses" by "pointing" to a transcendent divine confrontation with humanity. According to the new hermeneutic influenced by Heidegger, biblical revelation is to be put in the framework of a "language-event," or internal encounter, in which one experiences authentic being.

These and similar redefinitions of inspiration rest on the assumption that "the Living God does not speak his word to men in intelligible form" (p. 24). As we have seen, this assumption is contrary to the prophetic-apostolic witness of the Bible itself, represents a departure from the historic view of inspiration, and is destructive of the subject matter of valid theologizing. Henry quotes Pinnock who has said, "Wordless revelation . . . is mere mysticism" (p. 23).

D. The Nature and Scope of Inspiration

Inspiration is *that supernatural influence of the Holy Spirit whereby the sacred writers were divinely supervised in their production of Scripture, being restrained from error and guided in the choice of words they used, consistently with their disparate personalities and stylistic peculiarities.* God is the source of Holy Scripture; Christ Jesus is the central message; and the Holy Spirit, who inspired it and illumines its message to the reader, bears witness by this inscripturated Word to the Word enfleshed, crucified, risen, and returning (p. 25, italics his).

Thus begins one of the most incisive writings on the nature and scope of biblical inspiration. Henry asserts that, in one sense, Christianity is a book religion. And that book—the Bible—itself rules out any derivation from a latent divinity immanent in humankind. In fact, in biblical usage inspiration does not refer primarily to the writer but to the internal activity of the Holy Spirit and the outward result, the authoritative revelation.

The aim of the biblical writers is not to provide us with a textbook of science or history, or with a systematic exposition of moral philosophy or theology in the modern understanding, though scholars in these fields neglect it at the peril of truncated theories. The Bible is interpreted history, the concentration being on redemptive acts and their meaning.

Various misconceptions of modern humanity have militated against the acceptance of the inspiration of the Bible: the idea that the gospel narratives are theological fabrications representing apostolic apologetic interests, the notion that a book set in the cultural context of its time cannot convey transcultural truth, the bias against supernatural miracles, and the insistence that the presence of certain difficulties in the text involves writer errors in the autographs. But these misconceptions can be shown to be either self-contradictory or unfounded.

Following Warfield, Henry concludes by responding to four main formulas which biblical critics have employed to dilute the authority of New Testament teaching: (1) Christ's teaching versus that of the apostles; (2) apostolic ignorance or accommodation versus apostolic beliefs; (3) apostolic opinion versus apostolic teaching; and (4) biblical phenomena versus apostolic doctrine (i.e., infallibility in doctrinal but not historical or scientific matters). But these also can be shown to be implausible.

The truth is that everyone of us—non-theist and theist, philosopher and theologian, Catholic and Protestant, neo-Protestant and conservative evangelical—must come to the Scripture with the free subordination of all human thought to divine revelation. This is the beginning of true understanding and reliable exegesis. Conservatives can demonstrate the inadequacy of objections to inspiration; but, in the nature of the case, no one can demonstrate infallibility by piling up evidence and arguments for it "since historical and scientific verification are never absolute and do not go beyond probability" (p. 34). Logical dependence is just the reverse: "divine inspiration assures the inerrancy of what God inspires" (p. 35). In the end, the Word will judge us; we will not judge the Word. Therefore Jesus' exhortation, "They have Moses and the Prophets; let them hear them" (Luke 16:29). That exhortation was anticipated by Isaiah when he wrote, "To the law and to the testimony! If they do not speak according to this word, they have no [light of] dawn" (Isa. 8:20).

Conclusion

To be sure, the apologists of every generation (and we are told that a generation may narrow down to fifteen, ten or even five years or less) will be called upon to restructure and restate the case for biblical authority. We can be sure that, were Henry himself asked to write an introduction to the authority and inspiration of the Bible today, it would be somewhat different. But not so much so as some might think. Note some of the major characteristics of the treatment of the subject which we have just reviewed:

1) It assures us that the authority of Scripture is to be both affirmed and defended. The passivity of those who say that divine truth need not be defended but only proclaimed is rejected.

2) It does not overlook the challenge posed by the sacred writings of the world's great religions.

3) Its major propositions are consistently confirmed by resort to the testimony of Christ, the prophets and the apostles themselves.

4) Its argumentation is logical, rational, reasonable. But its position is not that of rational*ism*. Human reason does not sit in judgment upon divine revelation. Just the reverse.

5) It does not hesitate to deal with opposing views whether of cynical philosophers or skeptical theologians, neo-Protestants or misguided evangelicals.

6) It draws support, not only from Scripture, but also from the great minds, hearts and confessions of the church, past and present.

7) Its tone is as kindly and courteous as its argument is consistent and convincing.

Whatever form our apologetic for biblical authority may take in the future, let it do justice to the biblical teaching on inspiration and revelation and let it exhibit these characteristics.

Lesslie Newbigin is correct in stating that what is needed in our day is a new *arche* (starting point) for thought and that that *arche* is to be found in the Bible. He errs, however, when he goes on to state that it is restricted to biblical *events* which "form the substance of the Scriptures and which have their center and determining focus in the events concerning Jesus" (Newbigin 1991: 28). No, the Bible itself is fully authoritative. The Bible itself is the best interpreter of the Bible. In the Bible we have both the events *and* their interpretation. Words and meanings coincide. That is what inspiration secures (see Wells 1990: 161).

3

Erich Sauer:
Rediscovering Biblical Theology

"Theology is the queen of the sciences"; "All of our problems are theological"—dicta such as these have been rather widely accepted among Christians in the past. Moreover, curricula of our Bible colleges and seminaries have reflected that acceptance. Increasingly, however, the biblical/theological disciplines have been challenged by competing systems of knowledge, particularly the sociology of knowledge. Missiology itself has become more and more dependent upon the social sciences while its foundation in biblical revelation shows signs of gradual erosion (see Hesselgrave 1988: 131-46). Edward Rommen fears that missiology is being "detheologized" (Rommen 1994).

But that is not the end of the matter. In some church and mission circles the very word "theology" has the connotation of being impractical—a deterrent to spiritual experience and a roadblock to decisive action. We hear references to theology (and doctrine) as being "dead letter" and contrasted with the life-giving Spirit who effects personal holiness and spiritual power. But what is the Bible itself if not theology? And whose work is the Bible if not the work of the Spirit?

Etched in my memory is the statement of a young mission enthusiast addressing a conference on "unreached peoples." He said, "We are not going to muck around in theology while multiplied millions are going to hell without ever having heard of Jesus!" No matter that unless someone "mucks around" in theology—and does a good job of it—fewer and fewer church members will believe in either hell or the necessity of hearing about Jesus! Maturity has occasioned second thoughts on the part of my young friend and he now relates mission to the larger plan of God, but at the time neither he nor his hearers seemed bothered by his anachronistic statement.

Who? Me? A Theologian?

Thirty years ago John H. Gerstner wrote an insightful little book entitled *Theology for Everyman* (Gerstner 1965). The truth is that every person *can be* a theologian and every person who is saved *must be* a theologian (cf. Davis 1978: 23)! Why? Because theology has to do with a knowledge of God and his relationship with his creatures. Without it, there is no knowledge of God nor can there be a relationship with him. So to be a Christian one must be a theologian!

But what *kind* of theologian must one be? After all, there are various kinds of theologians—natural, apologetic, exegetical, biblical, systematic, historical, dogmatic, contextual and so on. Obviously "everyman" need not be any of these in the technical sense. But "everyman" can be a theologian in the sense of knowing what the Bible says about God, his purpose and plan, and his relationship with his creatures. In essence that is what biblical theology is all about. And biblical theology is the special focus of this chapter for three distinct reasons. First, along with exegetical theology it is foundational to other types of theology. Second, it has been sadly neglected even among those who hold to the complete authority of Scripture, often with disastrous results. Third, for reasons I hope to make crystal clear, it holds unusual promise for effective ministry in the postmodern world we are entering.

The Biblical Theology Movement

In a brief historical overview, G. Ernest Wright says that biblical theology developed in the late Reformation Period as a reaction to theologies based on church tradition and/or modern scholasticism. Initially it referred to teaching that is consistent with the Bible, but with the development of systematic theology, that broad definition would no longer do. At the end of the eighteenth century, Johann Gabler attempted a more refined definition. But, broadly or narrowly conceived, biblical theology was to come upon hard times as a result of nineteenth-century higher criticism (G. Ernest Wright 1991: 101). And so we come to the Biblical Theology Movement and the renaissance of biblical theology in the present century.

According to the Old Testament scholar Walter Kaiser (see Kaiser 1978: 1 ff.), the "golden age" of the Biblical Theology Movement began in 1933 with the publication of Walter Eichrodt's two-volume work on Old Testament theology. Within a generation, both the climax and the reversion of that movement into a "history of Israel's religion" type of study came with Gerhard von Rad's two volumes on Old Testament theology published in 1962 and 1965. It was then that Langdon Gilkey and James Barr pointed out that in those thirty years the Biblical Theology Movement had not progressed beyond the categories of the old German liberalism despite the use of biblical language. The Movement was in crisis. Some even pronounced it dead.

But exactly why?

Eichrodt had been right in the beginning when he observed that no theology is possible if Old Testament history does not provide some constant, normative concepts. Von Rad was correct in giving attention to the chronological development of the Old Testament and its message. The problem was that because of their prior commitment to modernism and the "assured results" of source criticism, the approach of Eichrodt, von Rad and their kind simply could not yield the theological constants Eichrodt himself said are necessary.

The historical-descriptive type of biblical theology espoused by von Rad and others had two major weaknesses. First, it often denied the objective nature of recorded events while still using biblical language. For example, proponents spoke of the "biblical acts of God" while at the same time denying the existence of miracles. In what sense, then, did God "act," and how are those "acts" to be understood? Von Rad's answer was clear but unacceptable. He said that the object of Old Testament theology was to ascertain what Israel professed about Yahweh. Israel's professions were not faith statements; they were *acts* by which the people expressed their awareness of a relationship with God. There was not, then, one Old Testament theology but a variety of Old Testament theologies. Implicit in von Rad's answer was the second major weakness of this approach. Namely, it highlighted what the text supposedly *meant* in Old Testament times while stopping short of saying what it *means* to us today.

The theological-normative type of biblical theology espoused early on by Eichrodt and others had emphasized the importance of discovering what the text *means,* but it also had major drawbacks. First, all too often it too denied the objective nature of recorded events. Second, in order to get to what the text *means* it resorted to a Kierkegaardian existential leap of faith. Third, the formulations of so-called normativity came from the ready-made formulations of systematic theology or from the theologian's personal modern framework. As Kaiser says, "The *then* of the ancient text suddenly became the *now* of the present reader's needs, with no one knowing how or by what process" (Kaiser 1978: 6; emphasis his).

Kaiser writes as an Old Testament theologian, but New

Testament and systematic theologies reveal parallel developments that we cannot pause to detail here. I recall the experience of a very bright university student in Kyoto, Japan, in
the early 1960s. Just prior to his conversion he had attended a
Bible class on the Book of Acts held at the university. He related how the instructor seemed embarrassed by the Acts' miracles and proceeded to explain them on natural grounds. For
example, when Eutychus fell from the third-story window in
Troas he did not die but had the wind knocked out of him.
Therefore he was not actually brought back to life but only re-
suscitated (Acts 20:7-12). On Malta a snake bit Paul's hand,
but it had been suddenly aroused from a deep sleep and therefore was without venom. So Paul was not really poisoned at all
(Acts 28:1-6). My student friend's ultimate evaluation of the
Bible class was to the effect that the only miraculous thing
about it was the instructor's ability to explain the text without
resort to divine intervention!

Interestingly enough, during a lecture series scheduled
at that same university and about the same time, Paul Tillich
confessed that if he had his life's work to do over, he would not
write a systematic theology but would devote his efforts to con-
structing a theology of the history of religion. He was that tak-
en up with Buddhist and other Oriental religious traditions.

Incidently, my Japanese student friend came to faith in
Christ and is today an outstanding pastor, the unbiblical theologies of his Acts mentor and Paul Tillich notwithstanding.

Biblical Theology that is Biblical

What exactly is biblical theology in the more narrow
sense of the term? What is distinctive about it? What method of
biblical theology distinguishes it from systematic theology or
the history of religion? What is its task?

First, its *definition*. For this we go back to G. Ernest
Wright, who says:

> It [biblical theology] describes God by recounting what God has done. It must be defined as the confessional recital of the acts of God in history, together with what must be inferred from those acts (Wright 1991: 101).

Wright's definition may be a good place to begin but, in the light of the preceding discussion, it obviously leaves the door open to the "history of Israel's religion" and "multiple theologies" approaches we have rejected. More must be said.

Secondly, what are some *distinctives* of biblical theology as we understand it? At the very least there are four distinctives:

1) *A unity of plan and purpose.* About the time the Biblical Theology Movement was gaining momentum, Geerhardus Vos wrote a book that answered the problem of multiple theologies in the Bible. In his book *Biblical Theology* (Vos 1948) he followed biblical revelation historically and attempted to show that all parts of Scripture come together in a unified theology and a unity of plan and purpose. That is certainly an important dimension of "biblical theology that is biblical." The Bible has a multiplicity and a diversity of authors, events and ideas. But at the same time, it has unity, a plan that is single and divine. Biblical theology emphasizes that unity.

2) *A chronological development.* Kaiser speaks of the "diachronic approach" to the biblical text, the chronological development of events and ideas. Though the arrangement of books in our Bible is not strictly a historical arrangement, an over-arching historical progression is evident. The divine plan is set out in "successive installments" (Kaiser 1978: 10-11).

3) *Narrative form.* Closely allied to chronological development is the narrative form of much of Scripture. There is one story, one history, here—"*His* story," with a beginning, a center and an end. And there are all sorts of "little stories" that fit into the one big story. Biblical theology highlights story.

4) *Objectivity and normativity.* Many of the events of Scripture challenge our credulity as moderns unless we are willing to lay aside our modernistic bias against direct divine intervention in human affairs. Nevertheless, if we understand the text on its own terms (which does not rule out dealing with editorial impositions based on real evidence rather than personal and cultural biases), it is clear that the writers intended their accounts to be taken at face value. The Bible contains what William Osborne calls "*historical* story" (Osborne 1993: 18-3, emphasis mine). In the words of David Wells,

> The importance of the story form in the Bible does not lie in the story form itself . . . . Its importance lies in the fact that as a narrative of God's acts in the external world, it has yielded truth that is as objective as the events to which it is wedded. It was this that was distinctive in the biblical period, and it is this that is decisive for ours (Wells 1992: 259).

Thirdly, what about *methodology?* Not all, even of those who are committed to this kind of biblical theology, will agree with every aspect of his approach, but Walter Kaiser's method seems difficult to improve upon:

> Our proposal is to distinguish sharply biblical theology's method from that of systematics or the history-of-religion. There is an inner center or plan to which each writer consciously contributed. A principle of selectivity is already evident and divinely determined by the rudimentary disclosure of the divine blessing-promise theme to all men everywhere as the canon opens in Genesis 1-11 and continues in Genesis 12-50. Rather than selecting that theological data which strikes our fancy or meets some current need, the text will already have set up priorities and preferences of its own. These nodal points can be identified, not on

the basis of ecclesiastical or theological camps, but by such criteria as: (1) the critical placement of interpretive statements in the textual sequence; (2) the frequency of repetition of the ideas; (3) the recurrence of phrases or terms that begin to take on a technical status; (4) the resumption of themes where a forerunner had stopped often with a more extensive area of reference; (5) the use of categories of assertions previously used that easily lend themselves to a description of a new stage in the program of history; and (6) the organizing standard by which people, places,   and ideas were marked for approval, contrast, inclusion, and future and present significance (Kaiser 1978: 11-12).

It is apparent that all of this relates intimately to the subject of biblical interpretation which is the topic of the next chapter. In the present context it is important to point out that this approach not only preserves the strengths and avoids the pitfalls of Biblical Theology Movement methodologies referred to above, it also reflects the distinctives of a "biblical theology that is biblical."

Fourth, what about the *task* of biblical theology? Commenting on the task, B. B. Warfield once wrote (as quoted in Davis 1978: 144-45):

The task of biblical theology, in a word, is the task of coordinating the scattered results of continuous exegesis into a concatenated   whole . . . . (144)

. . . .

It is to be hoped that the time will come when no commentary will be considered complete until the capstone [biblical theology] is placed upon its fabric . . . (144)

. . . .

Biblical theology is not . . . a rival of   systematics; . . . it is the basis and source of systematics (145).

The Biblical Theology of Erich Sauer

Of numerous theologians whom we could consider at this point (some of whom have developed more up-to-date and nuanced theologies), I choose to go back to a biblical theologian who did his thinking, writing and teaching during the early days of the Biblical Theology Movement but whose theology and methodology were intensely biblical.

I should also mention that, after arriving on the mission field in 1950, I perused my meager library for reading material and settled on three works of Erich Sauer—*The Dawn of World Redemption, The Triumph of the Crucified,* and *From Eternity to Eternity.* Having studied the works of various systematic theologians in seminary, especially the seemingly endless pages of super-fine print in A. H. Strong's *Systematic Theology,* Sauer's works became something of a theological and spiritual oasis. Here was a first-rate theologian, and a German theologian at that, who primarily interacted with the biblical text, not so much with the works of other theologians. Here was a theologian who not only *referred* to the Bible (there are 5,900 Scripture references in the first two volumes of the above-mentioned trilogy) but also *rehearsed* and *revivified* it. Among other things, Sauer's works confirmed the fact that I was engaged in an enterprise of such surpassing significance that it was conceived in the mind of God in eternity past and has been central to all his dealings with humankind from the very beginning. I needed that.

Sauer was the principal of Wiedenest Bible School in the Rhineland. The trilogy mentioned above appeared in German shortly after the close of World War II and was then translated into various languages, the English versions being translated by G. H. Lange and published in the United States in the early 1950s. The three volumes were celebrated by numerous scholars—F. F. Bruce, A. Rendle Short, G. H. Lange, and Professor Koberle among them. When writing the foreword to the English translation of the first volume of Erich Sauer's trilogy *(The Dawn of World Redemption)*, the late F. F. Bruce wrote:

> We have nothing quite so good, as far as I know, by way of a handbook of evangelical theology based, not on the logical sequence of most creedal statements and dogmatic treatises, but on the historical order exhibited by the Bible itself. The thoroughly biblical character of the whole work, in form as well as in substance, is a sheer delight (Bruce 1953: 7).

As I say, even more penetrating analyses of the Old Testament have been written since that time, but my point in quoting Bruce is to emphasize both the nature of biblical theology and Bruce's delight in reading it.

This first book in the trilogy, then, deals with the "Divine unfolding of salvation" from creation to Christ; the second with "the winning of the church, the conversion of the nations, the transfiguring of the universe " (Sauer 1952: 10). These two volumes were originally published as one book, and central to the whole is Christ and his redemption, the church and its calling, the Kingdom and its establishment, God and his glory. Sauer speaks of the unfolding of this divine plan in both the Bible and history as a "majestic divine symphony," with a theme and harmonious rhythm that progressively unfolds from beginning to end (Sauer 1951: 10 and 1953:12). The analogy is well taken because over and over Sauer returns to the divine plan theme in order to embellish and develop it. Increasingly the believing reader becomes persuaded that he or she dare not miss God's timing or be "out of tune."

The third book in the trilogy, *From Eternity to Eternity,* is somewhat different. It is divided into three parts, the first of which summarizes the material in the first two books but displays salvation history by following "longitudinally" through the centuries such streams as the methods of revelation, the history of Israel, the salvation of the nations, and the history of the Messiah. It is accompanied by a colored chart that depicts the progressive development of the redemptive plan of God. The last two parts of the book deal with the inspiration and authority of the Bible (upon which everything else stands or falls), and a justification for the expectation of an earthly kingdom (the millennium).

For anyone who accepts the authority of Scripture and is open to the Spirit, the ability of Sauer to dissect the sacred text and disclose the heart of God's plan for the world and its peoples is utterly compelling. Though the above quotations and synopses give indications of this, it may be helpful to provide some additional examples.

1) Highlighting the progressiveness of God's plan, Sauer writes:

> In Abram God chose a single person; in Jacob this grew to a family; at Sinai this became a nation. In the present age God is gathering to Himself a supernational people *out of* all nations . . . ; in the coming kingdom of God there will be a universal fellowship of peoples . . . . (Sauer 1953: 54; emphasis his).

2) With reference to the promise to Japheth ("Let him dwell in the tents of Shem"—Gen. 9:27), Sauer follows the history of peoples down to Paul and his vision of the man of Macedonia (Acts 16:9-10) by which God directed Paul to the west. He notes that this was about the time when Ming-ti, emperor of China, sent a mission to India which resulted in the entrance of Buddhism to China (A.D. 61-67). He then continues,

> But it is the incomparable significance of that dream-vision in Troas that with it the hour had struck for the bringing of the message of salvation over to Europe, so that now Japhetic Europe was appointed to be . . .

the citadel of the message of the kingdom of heavens (Sauer 1953: 79).

3) In dealing with Daniel's prophecies of world empires, Sauer reviews their actual development and demise and shows how the "will of the Divine World Ruler governed" so that Roman rule and civilization could play its part in the expansion of the church:

> *On account of Christ* Rome *had to* become that which it became. It is true that the Romans were "the robbers of the world," but without their knowledge their robberies played a part in the annals of salvation. Rome had to create a reservoir for human civilization in preparation for the spread of the gospel to mankind. Thus it was her task "to gather, or shall we say quite plainly, to gather for Christ" (Sauer 1953: 174; emphasis his).

4) Closing his first volume by expatiating on still other circumstances in the "fulness of the time" that presaged not only the coming of the Messiah but the spread of his gospel, Sauer underscores that "fulness" with numerous scintillating insights. Among them:

> It was through the service of converted Jews of the Diaspora, from Cyprus and Cyrene, that the Christian church in Antioch arose . . . . The Antioch of Antiochus, the "little horn," the "Anti-Christ" of the third world-empire (Dan. 8:9-14; 11:21-45)—here surprisingly enough was the starting point of the world mission of Christianity. What an irony of the Divine government of the world! (Psa. 2:4). Truly, "the Light shineth in the darkness" (John 1:5) (Sauer 1953: 179).

5) When opening a major section on the church in the

second volume of his trilogy, Sauer's very first word is on the "call" of the church. Concerning it he writes,

> Evangelizing is the greatest thing now going on in the world. It is a great power in servant's form.
>
> . . . .
>
> . . . the present work of God is "to take *out* of the nations a people for His name" (Acts 15:14), that is, not Christianizing the races but evangelizing the races for the purpose of calling out a *super*-national people of God (Matt. 28:19; Mark 16:15) (Sauer 1952: 58; emphasis his).

6) Writing about Paul and his missionary strategy, Sauer includes some nuances that would enhance the commentary of any missiologist. For example,

> . . . Paul's activities in the gospel could not have been planned in a more practical manner than they were. It is therefore just to speak of Paul's "missionary strategy." All is so systematic, . . . so planned in advance for the swiftest and most extensive spread of the gospel . . . .
>
> But with all this it was not Paul who planned but the Lord he served . . . . So that it is very just to speak of a missionary strategy in the life of Paul, but the strategy was not Paul's but Christ's, not of the ambassador but of the Sender, not of the herald but of the Lord of the enterprise. Christ was the Leader, Paul the agent; Christ was the Director, Paul the traveler; Christ was the Commander, Paul the soldier (2 Tim. 2:3; 4:2; 2 Cor. 6:7; Eph. 6:10-20) (Sauer 1952: 71-72).

7) Finally, Sauer speaks of a millennial condition in

terms that, though it will not meet with agreement among all students of prophecy, nevertheless demonstrates a sensitivity to the importance of "peoples as peoples" that contemporary missiologists especially will appreciate. He writes,

> The end will be the universal subjection of the world to Christ. . . . Thus it is a mission to mankind under the sceptre of the Almighty, world evangelization with Christianizing of civilization, the proclamation of the kingdom with the winning of all peoples. It is thus to be the most important and most real missionary period of history, and for the first time on earth there will be Christian nations and associations of peoples within the meaning of Holy Scripture (Isa. 45:22-24).
>
> The fact that peoples, as peoples, at this exact time turn to the Lord, and not as individuals only, as formerly, has its especial reason in this, that the nations will have seen with their eyes the mighty acts of God; the glorification of the church, Christ's coming in glory, the decisive battle at Har-Magedon, the judgment of the peoples in the valley of Jehoshaphat, God's salvation and wonders with Israel. "As the Lord will deliver the prisoners of Zion, we shall be as those who dream. . . . Then will one say among the heathen, The Lord has done great things for them" (Psa. 126:1, 2) (Sauer 1952: 165).

This does not do anything approaching justice to Erich Sauer's biblical theology. But if he was not a pioneer among twentieth-century theologians who rediscovered the potential of biblical theology for enlightening the church and infusing it with divine passion and purpose, he was at least within the vanguard of those who did so after the birth of the Biblical Theology Movement. Sauer keeps church and mission together. And he cradles both in the purpose and plan of a sovereign God.

Conclusion

From an anthropological as well as a distinctly Christian point of view, it is all but impossible to overestimate the significance of theology in general and biblical theology in particular. There is a consensus among most anthropologists that a cosmology or worldview is at the core of culture. It is out of that core that the rest of culture emanates.

The Christian anthropologist G. Linwood Barney has proposed a "four-layered" diagram of culture in which worldview (cosmology and basic belief system) is at the center (Barney 1978; see Figure 1).

Figure 1

LAYERS OF CULTURE

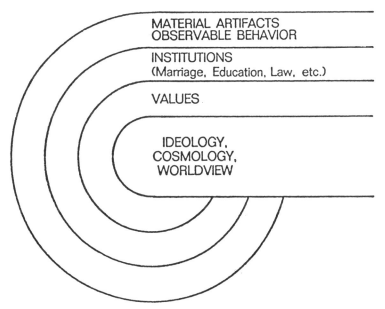

From a Christian perspective the important thing to learn from this is that change becomes more and more difficult to effect as one moves from the outer layers to the inner core. For example, it is much much easier to get a person to pray a certain prayer, go to church, or use prayer beads than it is to change his or her worldview. But true conversion first and foremost involves a change of worldview—adopting a completely different understanding of God and his world; of self, sin and salvation; and of the Christ who is both Savior and Lord. A change of behavior and even institutions without a change of values and worldview is not truly conversion. It is syncretism.

How are worldviews formed in the first place? Basically by the telling of a story (and stories within a story) and drawing inferences from it. That's why all peoples have their story (myth, legend, history—in one sense it makes little difference) and draw upon it to sustain their values, institutions and behavioral patterns. So the Japanese build upon the Shinto myth of Izanagi and Izanami and the Sun Goddess. Hindus build upon one or another version of the Golden Egg myth. In one way or another the Chinese build upon the story of Pan Ku. Post-Christian Westerners build upon the story of naturalistic evolution. Christians build on the biblical story.

How does the worldview change or "exchange" implicit in Christian conversion take place? How does one go about reconstructing a Christian worldview that has fallen upon hard times? Not first by stressing appropriate behavioral patterns or building Christian institutions. Not necessarily by enumerating Christian values or outlining the basics of a Christian worldview. Nor even by taking bits and pieces, the "little stories" of the Bible and dealing only with them. *Worldview change is best accomplished by studying and telling or retelling the biblical "big story" that enshrines the Christian worldview. That is why, as we will see later, some of the most successful Christian missionizing has been done by missionaries who resorted to telling the big story that unfolds from Genesis to Revelation. And that is why, in our own post-Christian culture "Walk*

Through the Bible," "Step by Step Through the Bible," the "Divine Drama," "Bible Panorama" and similar studies have become increasingly important to our own culture and churches. Thousands of American Christians who have attended church all of their lives are taking these "walks" or "journeys" through the Scriptures and then excitedly exclaiming "For the first time I understand the Bible!" and "I have never seen it this way before!"

It is at this point that I take somewhat of an exception to David Wells and others who seem to me to underrate the importance of the narrative form itself (cf. Wells 1992: 259). True, it is the *substance* of the Bible narrative that is most important. But the story *form* is also important because stories are the mode in which worldviews are best transmitted from generation to generation and from one people to another. Stories are readily told and easily remembered. And one's personal "little stories," whether of success or failure, are most readily understood and resolved in the light of the worldview "big story."

In subscribing to the right kind of biblical theology, then, there is a very real sense in which we subscribe to both the substance *of God's revelation and also to the* strategy *of it. We convey the* message *of the Bible, but we also communicate according to its* method. *The word "method," after all, is composed of the preposition* meta *("in the midst of" or "together with") and the noun* hodos *("way" or "journey"). "Method" is a "way one takes in the company of others." So, rightly conceived, to rediscover biblical theology is to* think *with God and then to* walk *with him; to join with him both in what is to be understood and the way in which it is to be communicated.*

4

William J. Larkin, Jr.:
Rethinking Bible Interpretation

One of the encouraging aspects of contemporary church life in North America is the renewed interest in the Bible. All across the continent people are meeting for Bible study. Some of them proceed *deductively*—that is, they assume a basic understanding of the teachings of Scripture which are then related to certain questions or problems, topics or proposals in accordance with the interests and objectives of the participants. The majority of them proceed *inductively*—that is, they approach the biblical text with an eye to discovering its meaning.

Certain traps are to be avoided when employing either of these methods of Bible study. When approaching the biblical text deductively, one must avoid the tendency to "proof-text"—to search out those passages that support one's position while overlooking passages that might be at odds with it. Almost all of the world's peoples are in danger of falling into this trap because all of us have a tendency to seek corroboration for what we already believe.

When approaching a passage inductively, one must try to avoid interpretations that may be appealing to the interpreter but are not warranted by a careful study of the text itself. We Americans are especially vulnerable at this point not only because in our hurried existence we often lack the patience required to learn principles of sound interpretation, but also because Western individualism tends to lead to a respect for every person's opinion no matter how ill-informed it might be. Group Bible studies often display this tendency. As Trevor McIlwain says,

> A common form of Bible study is to have each person give his own ideas about the portion of Scripture under consideration. When all the opinions have been voiced, the leader summarizes the different thoughts and interpretations (McIlwain 1991: 74).

As encouraging as the current Bible study movement is, therefore, its overall impact could be much greater if more attention were given to three things. First, church and mission strategy should make a much larger place for Bible studies within the program of the local church. Otherwise centers of evangelism, fellowship and spiritual growth will increasingly distance themselves from the local church and its influence. Second, of the various ways of going about Bible study, special consideration should be given to inductive and chronological studies in order to lay a foundation for understanding the plan and purpose of God in history. Third, a much higher priority should be given to instruction in principles of valid interpretation and application of the biblical text in order to avoid unbridled subjectivism. We must be careful lest we unwittingly approach the Bible in the same way as Hindus approach the Vedas, Shintoists approach the Kojiki, or Muslims approach the Qu'ran. Any one of a number of good books on biblical interpretation and the use of aids such as *The International Inductive Study Bible* (published by Harvest House Publishers) would be good places to begin.

Before concluding this chapter we will highlight some

basic principles of interpretation and application and relate them to future strategy. But first it is necessary to revisit some signposts along the "hermeneutical highway" of the past in order to help chart our course for the future.

Moderns and Meaning

By the time we had arrived at the middle of the twentieth century, it was apparent that centuries-old questions concerning the existence of God and the nature of truth and goodness were yielding to relativism and new questions. For the most part those new questions had to do with meaning—not just the meaning of words and things, but with the meaning of life and even the meaning of meaning. Apart from belief in God, the search for meaning became frustrating if not fruitless. Suzanne Langer found meaning in the fact that humanity is a "symbolizing creature" but admitted that this was an expression of her "faith." She could not really explain *why* humanity is different. Jean-Paul Sartre found no ground for meaning at all except what an individual insists upon as his or her meaning. Sartre ended up with solipsism and nihilism. By the 1960s and 1970s a significant part of Western society was "attending the Theater of the Absurd"!

Often leapfrogging over such fundamental problems, students of language and communication concentrated on another sort of inquiry. Since humans are communicating creatures, it is obvious that meaning of some kind exists, but where is it to be located and how is it to be determined? We have written rather extensively concerning this (cf. Hesselgrave 1991: 55-78) and will return to it briefly in the next chapter, but it is important to note that approaches to these problems have proved to be both diverse and divisive. For their part, classical and "new" rhetoricians have tended to accept traditional understandings of the relationship between words and meaning and have focused on the purposes of communication.

Literary critics have a special interest in literary genres and relate questions of meaning to types of language. Linguists can be expected to shy away from a word-centered view of meaning and concentrate on the interface or relationship between the various linguistic elements. Semanticists have tended to focus on the relationship between words and their referents, and on where meaning is to be found.

It goes without saying that the numerous intra- and inter-disciplinary debates that have occurred, extending into the last century and beyond, have had a profound effect on Christians and non-Christians alike.

Meaning and Sub-Orthodox Hermeneutical Methodologies

The traditional name of the discipline that deals with questions of biblical interpretation is "hermeneutics," though confusion often results from the fact that the term has a variety of meanings and usages. One source of confusion results from the fact that hermeneutics is often expanded to include exegesis. Understood more narrowly, however, exegesis has to do with determining the original meaning of the text (what it meant to people back in biblical times), while hermeneutics has to do with the present-day meaning of the text (what it means today or its *significance* for people today). Personally, I prefer to preserve this distinction but often bow to what seems to be more conventional—namely, a broader understanding of hermeneutics which includes both.

Hermeneutics derives its name from Hermes, the messenger god of ancient Greece. In that it is related to a pagan god, it is perhaps inappropriate to use it in relation to biblical interpretation. In that it is bequeathed by the Greeks, it is perhaps especially appropriate in the case of certain biblical scholars because, following the lead of some of the Greek philosophers and Renaissance and Enlightenment thinkers, they have insisted that unaided human reason is a sufficient guide to reality and meaning! Therefore, they have devised a method of biblical interpretation, the historical-critical method, whereby the content and meaning of Scripture is determined by "liberated" human reason and rationality. Let's see where that leads.

In the nineteenth century, Friedrich Schleiermacher's hermeneutic (the interpreter's preunderstanding, the dialectical "hermeneutical circle", grammatical and psychological analysis) was based on the notion that a word's meaning can only be understood in the context of what the interpreter already knows. Meaning is largely a matter of the subjective conditioning of the interpreter.

Ernst Troeltsch's historical-critical hermeneutic, on the other hand, was based on the notion that meaning is derived from a network of cause and effect that is traceable through a progression of contexts that ultimately encompasses all of history and reality. Interpretation is largely a matter of historical conditioning.

Those who took their principles of interpretation from either one or the other of these men logically concluded that even revealed truth can be communicated only in a relative, temporally conditioned form.

Early in this century Martin Heidegger emphasized tradition and the interplay between a traditional interpretation and the interpreter's relationship to tradition. The so-called "new hermeneutic" of people like Ernst Fuchs, Gerhard Ebeling and Krister Stendahl tends to follow Heidegger's lead. The question for them is, "How can a statement given to people in a specific historical context be the Word of God for us in our present and very different context?" As A. C. Thiselton indicates, they attempt to answer this question *deeply* and *creatively* but are less concerned with answering it *correctly* (Thiselton 1977: 323; for a full discussion see Elliott Johnson 1991: 63-65; 225-29).

Something similar could be said of the approach of James Barr who follows in the historical-critical train of Ernst

Troeltsch. He puts a great emphasis on the Bible as a record of what was believed in biblical times, but he also believes that the cultural and historical distance between "then" and "now" is too great to bridge by direct resort to the teachings of Scripture. The responsibility of the biblical interpreter is to interpret for the world what the church and Christians "mean today."

The neo-orthodox theology of scholars like Karl Barth, Emil Brunner and Hendrik Kraemer represented an effort to recover an authoritative Word of God in Scripture, but was too beholden to critical methodology as well as to Kierkegaardian existentialism. Neo-orthodoxy differentiated between the apostles' witness (normative in the sense that they were the first witnesses) and the contemporary witness of the Spirit (who makes the biblical witness become God's word for us today). Put very simply, in this understanding the biblical text is the Word of God only as the Holy Spirit makes it so to the reader/hearer/interpreter.

Skeletal though it is, it will be apparent from this overview of some major hermeneutical developments of the past that they often share one fundamental weakness. However they may approach Scripture and arrive at some allegedly relevant meaning for people today, they betray a debt to higher criticism and as a result undercut the absolute authority of Scripture in their very methodology. There are various kinds of relativism, but a relativism that undercuts the full authority of Scripture cannot serve as a corrective to the afflictions of any person—premodern, modern or postmodern.

Meaning, Hermeneutics and Conservative Evangelicals

In the light of the kind of developments we have just sampled, the concerns of conservative evangelicals have shifted somewhat over the last generation. Increasingly the focus on biblical inspiration and inerrancy has been augmented by attention to matters of biblical interpretation and application. Differences among evangelicals in matters of exegesis and hermeneutics have become just as pronounced (perhaps even more pronounced!) than those that surfaced in the inerrancy debates of twenty-five years ago.

First, evangelicals who have stood for the inerrancy and full authority of the Bible, such as Carl F. H. Henry, Kenneth Kantzer, Walter Kaiser, Gleason Archer and Norman Geisler, begin with the affirmation that truth and meaning are intimately related, and that "true statements are those that correspond to the facts, to reality, and the Bible communicates just such true verbal propositions" (Larkin 1993: 89). Others who still lay claim to being evangelical define truth in terms of faithfulness or being without deception. They hold that, even if the Bible is historically or scientifically inaccurate in certain places, "in the biblical understanding of the term, the Bible does not err. It is faithful—that is, not 'swerving from the truth and upsetting the faith'" (Larkin 1993: 90; quoting Gerrit C. Berkouwer). It is not easy to understand how those who hold to this latter position can lay claim to being evangelical in the historic and theological sense of the word. In any case, it is obvious that a difference as profound as this has serious implications when it comes to interpreting and applying Scripture.

Second, evangelicals differ with one another when it comes to semantics. Walter Kaiser more or less assumes referential or traditional sign theory. Anthony Thiselton subscribes to the conventional or functionalist approach to language. Robert Longacre finds evidence of the *imago Dei* in the "deep structures" associated with structuralism. John Feinberg concludes that no single theory will do and that something can be learned from various theories. There is much to be said for this sort of eclecticism, particularly if pitfalls as well as potentials are clearly pointed out.

Third, evangelicals differ as to the importance of literary genre in interpreting Scripture. The traditional distinction between teaching sections where truth can be directly applied and historical sections from which only principles are derivable has yielded to more complex distinctions. For example, Gordon Fee believes that the lack of educational opportunities in ancient times explains in part Paul's prohibition against women teaching in the church (1 Tim. 2:9-15). Larkin, on the other hand, says that this breaks down the distinction between teaching sections of the Bible (where teaching can be directly applied today) and historical sections (from which only principles are derivable). Making the teaching genre of the epistles into a kind of occasional literature is to undermine the universal normativeness of that part of the Bible where teaching is most consistently found (Larkin 1993: 94-95).

Fourth, differences are evident when it comes to the relationship between "meaning then" and "meaning now." Anthony Thiselton believes that the right kind of engagement between the interpreter and the text will result in a "fusion" of these two horizons. Walter Kaiser insists that there is a single meaning of Scripture, and that once the author's intended meaning is determined exegetically, that meaning can be essentially restated at any time and in any culture. In view of the profusion of meanings (significances) and even meaning types assigned to the biblical text these days, it is difficult to accept any approach that does not assign first priority to the intention of the Spirit-inspired author of the text.

One might gather from these and still other internal squabbles among evangelicals that the movement is in disarray and even in process of splintering. Some have concluded that that indeed is the case. Others point to a general and abiding commitment to the complete authority of Scripture and the underlying perspicuity or clarity of the biblical text and conclude that the movement will remain intact.

The jury is still out. Larkin feels that recent writings by Anthony Thiselton, Moises Silva, Vern Poythress, Gordon Fee and Millard Erickson are less reassuring at certain points. The writings of Carl Henry, Walter Kaiser, Grant Osborne, Elliot Johnson, and a new work by William Klein, Craig Blomberg and Robert Hubbard (1993) are more reassuring.

William J. Larkin, Jr., and His Biblical Theology of Hermeneutics and Culture

During the last generation there have been so many Bible-believing scholars who have tackled the really tough exegetical and hermeneutical problems to which we have referred that one is at a loss to know how best to single out one as a model for Bible study at home and abroad. Of several quite recent volumes to which I have already referred and which I have quite carefully reviewed, I have chosen to present William J. Larkin's model here, primarily because of the way in which he weds his concern for a biblical approach to questions of interpretation on the one hand, and his concern for positive outcomes for churches and missions in other cultures on the other. As a matter of fact, I acknowledge a debt to Larkin's work for some of what appears above as well as that which is to follow.

William Larkin, Jr., is a professor at Columbia Biblical Seminary and Graduate School of Missions. His original intention was to co-author a book on hermeneutics with Robertson McQuilkin, former missionary to Japan and subsequently president at Columbia. Circumstances were such that Larkin proceeded on his own with McQuilkin's encouragement and blessing. Thus *Culture and Biblical Hermeneutics— Interpreting and Applying the Authoritative Word in a Relativistic Age* (Baker 1988; University Press of America reissue in 1993) is the result of his own tireless and careful labors.

As the subtitle indicates, Larkin's work is a response to the challenges of pluralism and relativism that manifest themselves not only in the way secularists approach questions of truth and goodness, but also in the way in which many Christian scholars approach the Scriptures. By way of response, Larkin sets himself to two major tasks. First, he traces the historical background of developments in hermeneutics and the state of these discussions up to the early 1980s. Second, he develops a biblical theology of hermeneutics and culture, and then sets forth hermeneutical guidelines for interpreting and applying the Bible, suggests steps for a Bible study method, and provides examples from both Western and Third World cultural contexts.

Because of the nature of the present treatment, we will limit our focus to Larkin's guidelines, steps and examples. But the reader should be aware of the fact that this section of the book constitutes but nineteen pages of a book of 401 pages (with indices) of meticulously developed materials. Larkin actually submitted relevant parts of the text to about fifty authors in order to assure himself and his readers that he had been faithful to their position! The reader should also be aware of the fact that, though Larkin does distinguish between exegesis, hermeneutics and contextualization at one level, at another level the single term hermeneutics is inclusive of all three endeavors along with their subsidiary tasks.

Larkin's Guidelines for Biblical Interpretation and Application

Larkin's method of interpretation and application "moves back and forth between the part and the whole, the text and the various contexts in which it is to be understood" (Larkin 1993: 325). It involves four major steps—a preliminary one (overview)—and analysis, interpretation and application. Each major step entails certain "sub-steps."

The First Step: Overview

1) *Biblical Pre-understanding*. Adopt a biblical pre-understanding; pray for Holy Spirit illumination; take the stance of faith toward Scripture; and assume a humble, re-

pentant and teachable attitude. For example, each time one approaches the Scripture he or she should take time to thank God for the spiritual understanding that is one of the benefits of regeneration.

2) *Preliminary Study of the Text in Context.* Study the text in literary and historical context to determine the basic message in relationship to its immediate context, the particular book, Scripture as a whole, and the historical circumstances surrounding its writing. For example, the knowledge that the Thessalonian church was composed largely of Gentile believers of Greek extraction helps one understand the need to clarify the relationship between Christ's second coming and the resurrection of dead saints (1 Thess. 4:13-18). Why? Because, resurrection not being a part of the Greek worldview, it was hard for the Thessalonian church to comprehend.

3) *Cultural Pre-understanding.* Think about those elements in your culture that could be used to transmit the text of the message, what needs correction in your culture, and the significance of the biblical message for the worldview, social structures and behavioral patterns of your culture. Western "big bang" theory, for example, posits the notion that the universe had a beginning at one finite point in time. At this one point at least it is congruent with Scripture. African myths that describe a Supreme Being as withdrawing because of human misbehavior has its parallel in Genesis 2-3. At the same time there are differences that must not be overlooked in both cases.

Step Two: Analysis

1) *Grammatical Analysis.* Analyze the grammatical structure of the passage and determine what the various features contribute to its meaning. Most every schoolchild, for example, has had practice in diagramming sentences. This is more than a school exercise, it is a part of the inquiry into meaning.

2) *Literary Analysis.* Analyze the literary structure,

forms and figures of speech that are used to communicate the writer's meaning. Recognized literary conventions such as structure (word order, repetition, etc.) and genre (history, parables, figures of speech, etc.) mightily affect meaning. Jesus' word, "If your right eye makes you stumble, tear it out and throw it from you" (Matt. 5:29) is a hyperbolic way of showing the seriousness of sinful sexual thoughts. Other biblical passages reinforce the fact that it is not to be taken literally (e.g., Matt. 5:28 and 1 Cor. 6:13).

3) *Historical-Cultural Analysis*. Analyze word meanings in the light of historical-cultural information and the historical situation described in the text. Look first for meanings of words in the biblical context. In ancient Greek usage, *diatheke* means "a last will and testament"; but, informed by the Septuagint translation practice, it becomes clear that in the New Testament it means "the divine covenant" (cf. Isa. 59:21 in the LXX and Luke 22:20).

The Third Step: Interpretation

1) *The Biblical Context*. In the analysis step, the passage was taken apart. Now put it together, state the basic point, and make an exegetical outline that reflects both content and progression of thought. Relate the message of the text to the immediate context and book in which it is located. Trace the teaching of the passage to parallel passages of Scripture. For example, Jesus uses the term "Son of man" in various texts in the Gospel of Mark. Of various parallel passages, the proper background seems to be Daniel 7:13 where "one like the son of man" approaches the Ancient of Days and is given such authority, glory and power that all peoples worship him. The various Marcan passages in which Jesus uses this phrase seem to point to one or another of these attributes as when Jesus claims the authority to forgive sins when healing the paralytic (Mark 2:5).

2) *The Contemporary Cultural Context*. Interpreters must do the following: communicate through the respondents'

worldview and language stock (theirs or that of their audience); correct those parts of the worldview, structure and behavior that the Bible judges false; and introduce the signifi-cance of the message for the culture. For example, as relates to communication, the locus of meaning is to be found in the writer's intent concerning an extralinguistic referent. Therefore the interpreter has to find words in the language of the receptor culture that point to the same referent and communicate the sense of the text. The Old Testament, for example, commands children to "honor" their parents (Ex. 20:12). The New Testament echoes the same principle in Matthew 15:3-6 and Ephesians 6:1-3. The question is, does this refer to the same principle expressed in Asian—and particularly Confucian—cultures that stress filial piety (*hisao* in Chinese)? The answer is that there is a similarity but also a significant difference. Larkin points to the fact that filial piety in the Confucian sense is not just ethical but also religious and as religion it culminates in ancestor worship. He quotes Wang Chih-hisin: "The Jews look upon God as Father; the Chinese regard parents as God" (Larkin 1993: 349). Both the similarity and the difference must be taken into account.

The Fourth Step: Application

Biblical principles and commands are to be implemented in ordinary individual lives today. But how?

1) *Locating Normative Biblical Content*. Application of the biblical teaching should be *direct* by using both the biblical form and meaning or *indirect* by linking meaning with a culturally relevant form. There are three criteria for determining whether or not a given biblical teaching calls for *indirect* application. First, when the direct recipient of the teaching is limited by cultural context. Compare Jesus' general call for discipleship in Luke 9:23 with his specific instruction to the rich young ruler in Matthew 19:21. Second, when specific historical or cultural conditions indicate that a limited application was in-

tended. Some missiologists, for example, believe that baptism was just a culturally-relevant form of initiation rite and have wondered whether getting out of a casket would be more appropriate in our culture. And so on. Larkin, however, believes that the universal setting of the Great Commission indicates otherwise. Third, when a limited cultural rationale makes it clear that the writer intended to limit the extent of application. Some (most?) interpreters believe that the rationale for stipulations concerning women's head covering and hair in 1 Corinthians 11:2-16 is limited because Paul appealed to the custom of churches in general at that time. Larkin himself thinks that Paul's use of the phrase "the churches of God" and other factors indicate that the rationale is not limited and the instructions have universal application for women involved in worship leadership.

2) *Identifying the Contemporary Situation.* Interpreters must study the current context (their own, or another) to determine whether or not circumstances are appropriate for the application of a given command, promise or principle.

3) *Developing the Response.* What changes in thought, attitude or behavior are called for? Larkin uses the prohibitions against honorific titles in Matthew 23:7-10 as an example. He says: "Except in the case of "rabbi," the form of the command does not involve limiting cultural conditions and is therefore normative" (Larkin 1993: 358). Other passages recognize the position of teachers and even fathers, but in no place does the Bible link honorific titles with a person's name. The appropriate designation is "brother" (cf. Acts 9:17).

It will be immediately apparent from Larkin's illustrations above that not all interpreters will agree, even when following the same guidelines. Perhaps that is just as well. As long as Scripture is authoritative, as long as valid principles of interpretation and application are applied, and as long as this is done in the context of the church past and present, unity can prevail even when uniformity is not possible.

Conclusion

There can be no doubt that Bible-believing Christians face many challenges in a radically relativistic, religiously pluralistic and multicultural postmodern world. Not the least among them are those that have been made apparent in this chapter. Time has already demonstrated that Carl F. H. Henry was something of a prophet when over a decade ago he wrote:

> The problem of biblical authority will probably continue to disturb evangelicals very deeply. The issue will focus not simply on inerrancy, but also on interpretation as well, and especially on the culture-relatedness and culture-dependence of biblical revelation. Evangelicals insist that although the Bible was written in particular historical and cultural milieus, it speaks with binding authority to our different historical and cultural situations (*Christianity Today* 1981: 323 as quoted in Larkin 1993, 24).

Agreed. And Henry's statement will be for us more than a (true) prophecy. It will also serve as a bridge to our next chapter on culture and contextualization.

Before moving on, however, it might be well to point out that there is a certain lacuna in much of even the best of conservative evangelical hermeneutical writings. It has to do with the lack of what may be called a "missionary hermeneutic." It is important to recognize that attention to the role of culture in interpreting Scripture and communicating its message to the nations is not the same as attention to the mission itself. As we saw illustrated in the biblical theology of Erich Sauer, attention to, and interaction with, the Word of God should lead us to both a realization and an explication of God's great plan to include representatives of the various peoples of the world in his eternal family—and to his desire to use us in the fulfillment of that plan!

5

Paul G. Hiebert:
Revisiting Contextualization

It may be apocryphal, but the story is told of a famous American evangelist who was scheduled to preach in India. He asked the late D. T. Niles what he should do in order to adapt to an Indian audience. Niles is reported to have answered in the following vein:

> There is not too much that you can do. The Indian Holy Man is a mendicant who is unshaven, unkempt and unsightly because he has forsaken this world and its attachments. To most Indians you will appear to be more like a Madison Avenue materialist. But you cannot do much about that. So my advice is that you preach the gospel as best you can and let us interpret it for our people.

Of course, there are many religions, languages and subcultures in India. But, given the prevailing Hindu worldview, how is the gospel most effectively communicated in that context? That's a good question with which to begin a discussion of contextualization because the Hindu worldview and Hindu religiosity are about as divergent from our own as one can imagine. At the same time, Hinduism is a primary source of much of New Age thinking and the kind of pluralism and inclusivism that pervades postmodern Western thought.

Contextualization: A New Word

Though the word contextualization is relatively new, it is not entirely so. Having been coined in the early 1970s, it will soon have been in circulation for a generation—quite long enough to merit at least some consideration on the part of anyone who is serious about the church and its mission in the world. In fact, contextualization has been such a "hot" topic during the last twenty years that almost everyone in the church will at least be acquainted with the word.

At the same time, some measure of confusion concerning the subject is entirely understandable. Ralph Winter says that the word contextualization is a dangerous word (Winter 1993: 27-1). He is right. Contextualization was not much beyond its christening when it became the inheritor of a wide variety of definitions, explanations, evaluations and predictions. Encumbered by so much baggage at such an early age, the word contextualization could not be allowed to stand alone. It required the support of a variety of modifiers. Contextualization became true or false, good or bad, authentic or unauthentic, biblical or unbiblical, orthodox or liberal, prophetic or apostolic, effective or ineffective and so on. Of course, at one time or another most of these modifiers have also been applied to older semantic cousins such as indigenization, adaptation and accommodation. But in the case of contextualization, the definitions supplied by its originators were so biased in the direction of theological liberalism or neo-orthodoxy that some conservatives felt duty-bound to reject it altogether while others went to considerable lengths to redeem and refashion it. By the same token, liberals felt obliged to defend it. Confusion, then, is both understandable and defensible. But it should not be allowed to continue. This is a good time to revisit the concept.

Contextualiztion: An Old Idea?

Though it is widely recognized today that to be understood and effective gospel communication must take into account the dramatic changes that have occurred within Western cultures themselves, sensitivity to the requirements occasioned by cultural differences first surfaced among missionaries working with non-Western peoples. Well known are the debates engendered by the approaches of seventeenth-century Jesuits such as Matteo Ricci in China and Robert de Nobili in India. Ricci attempted to overcome Chinese opposition by identifying Christianity with Western technology and by accommodating ancestor worship. De Nobili opposed a total break with Indian caste and custom on the part of converts—a break which had automatically consigned Indian believers to untouchable status. He viewed caste as little more than social convention and urged Indian Christians to maintain their caste identification and live accordingly.

The debates within Catholicism that resulted from these approaches lasted for more than a century and, fueled by the opposition of other Catholic mission orders to de Nobili's methods especially, culminated in a repudiation of the Jesuits by Rome.

Of course, Protestant missionaries faced problems of their own. While some of them went about the task of raising up Christian communities separated from their surrounding culture as much by Western forms as by the requirements of the gospel itself, others attempted to learn as much of the local culture as possible in order to make appropriate adjustments. The members of the famous Serampore Trio—Carey, Marshman

and Ward—were not above criticism by some English supporters who complained that they gave too much attention to Indian
religion and culture. Some supporters went so far as to inquire
whether they had gone to India to convert Indians or to be converted by them!

Another facet of the tension between Christianity and
cultures became apparent in the middle of the nineteenth century. When the missiologist Rufus Anderson assessed the results of several decades of labors on the part of American missionaries, he concluded that if they were suddenly withdrawn
national churches would be hard pressed to survive. Anderson
and Henry Venn of England are credited with initiating the "indigenous church" theory—the idea that the objective of missions should be to establish churches that have native leadership and are firmly rooted in the soil of the local culture. In
the late nineteenth and early twentieth centuries, Anglo-
Catholic Roland Allen encouraged missionaries to follow the
example of Paul by handing the work over to converts as soon
as possible. This, he argued, would diminish foreign influence,
inhibit institutional growth, and allow native churches to grow
spontaneously under the direction of the Holy Spirit.

Enter Contextualization

We have written elsewhere concerning the genesis of
contextualization and have attempted to delineate its pitfalls
and potential (cf. Hesselgrave and Rommen 1989). It is not
necessary to repeat all of that here. However, it is important
that we review the basics.

In the years prior to the debut of contextualization, it
became apparent that the older terms were in trouble. Adaptation and accommodation smacked of "caving in" to culture. As
usually defined (self-support, self-governance, self-propagation),
indigenization was both theologically and culturally inadequate. All three terms seemed to suggest that missionaries are

somehow above culture and possess perfect knowledge of the gospel and church. That the interanimation between gospel, language and culture was much more tenuous and complex than most missionaries had thought became evident from the writings of Eugene Nida, William Reyburn, Jacob Loewen and others. Enter contextualization.

Implying as it does some kind of adjustment to the cultural context of respondents, contextualization could have been a relatively neutral term theologically. However, the interests of Nikos A. Nissiotis, chairman of a consultation on "Dogmatic or Contextual Theology" held in Bossey, Switzerland, in 1971, reflected a strong theological bias that was to prevail from the very first discussions on the subject. Nissiotis circulated a letter in which he wrote that the rise of technological society had the effect of leading to

> a kind of "contextual or experiential" theology which gives preference, as the point of departure for systematic theological thinking, to the contemporary historical scene over the biblical tradition and confessional statements constructed on the basis of the biblical texts, taken as a whole and thus used uncritically (quoted in Fleming 1980: 6).

Beginning with the "contemporary historical scene" in whatever continent, country or culture, contextualizers soon reinforced or inaugurated a number of theologies that gave priority to the interests and values of certain cultures and subcultures—Black Theology, Feminist Theology, Water Buffalo Theology, Theology of the Pain of God, Third Eye Theology, Theology of Ontology and Time, and so on. Most important among these theologies were the various forms of Liberation Theology which usually reflected the Marxist leanings of its formulators as well political and other struggles within their respective societies.

It should be made clear that the cultural preferences and

social concerns that gave rise to these theologies were for the most part legitimate. Our quarrel is not with the sensitivity of theologizers to those concerns. *Rather, it is with a contextualization meaning and method that gives priority to those concerns and relegates the Bible, the biblical Christ, and biblical doctrine to a secondary position in theologizing. When that happens, the Bible loses its authority and merely provides appropriate "reference points" and pertinent paradigms.* In Liberation Theology, for instance, the central biblical paradigm is the Exodus and Christ is portrayed as the Liberator par excellence. Liberation Theology has proved to be Bible-related but not Bible-based.

Already in the 1970s conservative evangelicals were reacting to ecumenical proposals both individually and collectively. Under the auspices of the Lausanne Committee for World Evangelization, thirty-three scholars and practitioners met in Willowbank, Bermuda, in 1978 to study issues relating to the gospel and culture. Willowbank papers were first assembled and made available by the Lausanne Committee and then published in 1979 in a volume edited by John Stott and Robert T. Coote (Stott and Coote 1979). Already at Willowbank it was apparent that there were significant differences among evangelicals themselves. Papers by Bruce Nicholls of India and Charles Kraft of Fuller Seminary, for example, revealed very divergent views on the nature of biblical revelation. Nicholls propounded a "dogmatic contextualization" that took biblical inerrancy and authority seriously while retaining a sensitivity to cultural differences. Charles Kraft proposed a "dynamic-equivalence transculturation" that viewed the biblical text as being much more culturally conditioned.

Since Willowbank, numerous evangelical theologians, biblical scholars, linguists, anthropologists, missiologists and practitioners have joined the discussion on contextualization. The writings of scholars such as Donald Carson, Harvie Conn, Charles Taber, Paul Hiebert, William Dyrness, and Edward Rommen have clarified many issues, but to this point have not mitigated problems and differences. The same could be said of important contributions made by evangelical scholars of the Third World.

Paul Hiebert's
"Critical Contextualization"

Paul G. Hiebert was born of Mennonite missionary parents in Shamshabad, A.P., India. He received his graduate training in missions at the Mennonite Brethren Biblical Seminary in Fresno, California, and his Ph.D. in anthropology from the University of Minnesota. He and his wife Frances served as missionaries in India for five years. From 1965 to the present he has taught at two state universities in Kansas and Washington and at two seminaries—Fuller Theological Seminary and Trinity Evangelical Divinity School. Currently he is Chairman and Professor of Mission Anthropology and South Asian Studies at the latter institution.

In an early monograph entitled "Critical Contextualization," Hiebert attempted to chart a path through the vagaries and extremes that tended to characterize discussions on contextualization from the beginning (Hiebert 1982). Opting for a position that Donald McGravran used to refer to as a "high view" of both the Bible and culture, he demonstrated a concern for both faithfulness to Scripture and "fitfulness" to culture.

Hiebert diagrammed approaches being taken to contextualization as in Figure 2 (Hiebert 1982: 290).

For purposes of illustration, Hiebert begins with certain questions posed by new high caste converts of a South Indian village—questions having to do with the suitability of Indian customs like wearing *tikkas* (spots on the forehead), footwashings at weddings, and participation in Hindu funerals.

One extreme response is to brand all such practices as unbiblical and pagan and therefore to reject them out of hand. In effect, this amounts to a wholesale rejection of contextualization. This response is bound to fail. Either the gospel will be rejected as foreign, or old customs and beliefs will go underground for a time only to emerge later in some kind of syncretism.

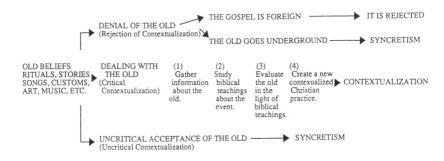

Another extreme response is to value the cultural heritage of India so highly that traditional ideas and practices are accepted into the church uncritically. This response is seriously flawed also. It grows out of a cultural relativism that destroys all authority and also opens the door to an inevitable syncretism.

"Critical contextualization" avoids both uncritical rejection and uncritical acceptance. It insists that old beliefs and customs first be examined to determine their meanings and functions in the society and, then, their acceptability in the light of biblical norms. It is essential that every church—whether in the East or the West—be led to do this, and that they do it in a certain way.

First, church leaders have the responsibility to make the

church aware of those areas of belief and life that call for a biblical critique. In India it may be the wedding ritual in which parents of the bride wash the feet of the groom. In America it may have to do with dating practices that often precede marriage.

Second, the pastor or missionary should lead the church in a discussion of the meaning of every aspect of the custom or belief in question. This must be done in a nonjudgmental way so that people will not feel threatened.

Third, the pastor or missionary should lead in a study of relevant biblical texts. Sound principles of Bible study should be demonstrated, but laity should take an active part in this study.

Fourth, the believers should be led in an evaluation of the custom or belief in the light of Scripture and make a decision concerning it. Leaders often make mistakes; the freedom to make mistakes must also be allowed to laity.

Fifth, new symbols or practices that convey Christian/ biblical meanings may be inaugurated.

Hiebert's monograph drew attention to certain theoretical and theological considerations that he subsequently dealt with in more detail. They constitute some of the "sticky wickets" with which contextualizers must come to terms. We might like to skirt them completely in a discussion of this kind, but to bypass them completely would be to do both Hiebert and the subject of contextualization an injustice. First, then, we go to theoretical complications. After that to theological foundations.

Theoretical Complications: Hiebert on Sign Theory

In two of his writings especially, Hiebert has attempted to work through certain thorny questions having to do with the nature of signs—questions that have been answered differently and have resulted in very diverse contextualization attempts even among evangelicals who hold to a high view of Scripture (Hiebert 1989 and 1994). Hiebert takes a third and mediating position as an alternative to two commonly held but extreme views

1. Positivism: Signs Equal Reality

One view of the nature of signs and the relationship between signs and reality, and, therefore, forms (words, rituals, drama, customs, etc.) and meaning is that they "equal each other" (see Figure 3). This view was taken by logical positivists,

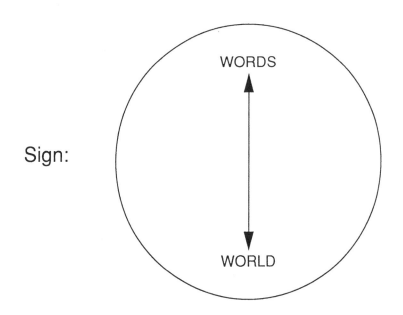

especially Rudoph Carnap and the members of the Vienna Circle, who attempted to make all language as exact as mathematical "language" and subject to verification by scientific method. Statements having to do with the supernatural or metaphysical could not be verified in this way and were therefore meaningless nonsense.

Of course, Christians could not follow positivists in reaching this conclusion, but many could and did subscribe to a more or less one-to-one relationship between signs and reality, or form and meaning. For them, the English word "tree," for example, meant the same thing as the Telegu word *"chetu."* Given that perspective, communication became "sender oriented." Translators tried to find the "exact" word or phrase to fit the original. Missionaries memorized the "right" way to say this or that. Once "correctness" was achieved, the responsibility to get the "true meaning" out of what was transmitted shifted from the sender to the receptors. The missionaries' rsponsibility was to preach as much as possible, get out as many Bibles and tracts as possible, etc. By the same token, since the meaning of the words and customs connected with pagan religions is somehow inherent in those words and customs, they were rejected forthwith. This is more or less the understanding that is behind the non-contextualized approach to communication and mission. Hiebert rejects it.

Sign:

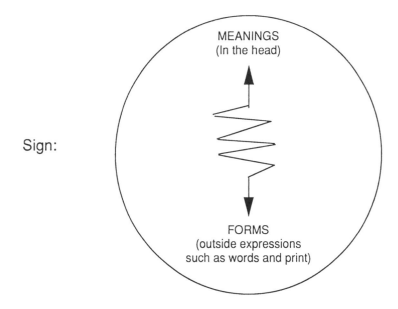

MEANINGS
(In the head)

FORMS
(outside expressions
such as words and print)

2. Instrumentalism (or Pragmatism): The Dyadic View

Another and almost opposite understanding of the nature of signs was informed by linguists, especially Wilhelm von Humboldt and his student Ferdinand de Saussure in the nineteenth century (see Figure 4). The former distinguished between the "inner" and "outer" aspects of language. The latter transformed that distinction into the "form" and "meaning" of a sign. This led to a dyadic view: signs have two parts—one exterior and objective, and the other interior and subjective. One part is internal—"in the head" and subjective. The other is external—"out there" and objective. The linkage between the two is arbitrary—a matter of convention. Either or both "tree" and "*chetu*" could be "bork" or whatever.

The consequences of this view among contextualizers has been profound. It has led to receptor-oriented communication. It has given rise to "dynamic equivalent" translations of the Bible in which words/forms are readily changed in order to "preserve" meaning. It has encouraged gospel communication that thinks of words/forms only as a means of "impacting" hearers. The translator/missionary/preacher's responsibility is somehow to get "into the heads" of the original hearers/readers, determine their thoughts and reactions, and then use words/forms designed to occasion similar thoughts and reactions in the minds of their respondents. It has also led to uncritical acceptance of even questionable customs of other cultures. Subjectivity, relativism and over-contextualization result from this view. Hiebert does not accept it.

3) The View of "Critical-Realism"

Hiebert credits an American mathematician and linguist, Charles Peirce, with introducing a third way of looking at signs—the way of "critical realism" (see Figure 5). In this view

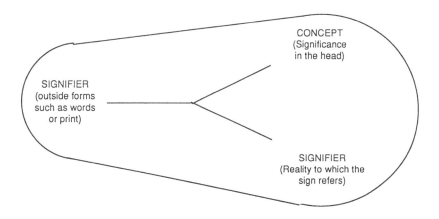

each sign links not two but three elements: the form (e.g., the word, object, event, etc.), the mental concept or image, and the reality referred or pointed to (the referent). Meaning, then, is neither in the word/form nor is it in the person/mind. It is in the correspondence between the inner idea or image and the outer reality. For English speakers, the word "tree" evokes the mental image of a tree and also refers to trees in the forest. For Telegu speakers, the word *"chetu"* serves the same purpose. However, as the words in the two languages are different, just so the images evoked by the two words may vary depending upon the American and Indian "tree/forest realities." If we want to, we can even manipulate and combine words to "create" new realities. For example, "purple cow" (remember, Hiebert is from India!) can be imagined because we have seen both the color purple and cows. That being the case, we can set out to paint a cow purple if we wish (don't even think of doing it in India, however!).

This is Hiebert's view and its implications for contextualization are far-reaching. Hiebert says:

> We cannot in all cases simply change meanings while retaining old forms. We need to examine carefully the nature of signs in the gospel—in Scripture, rituals and Christian life—in order to determine the extent to which they can be changed to fit another culture. We need also to examine the nature of signs in the culture in which we want to communicate the gospel to see if they can be used or changed to convey the message of the gospel (1994: 11-12).

Now if one reviews Hiebert's steps in doing contextualization in the church, it will become apparent that his approaches to sign theory on the one hand and to "critical contextualization" on the other are not only compatible but also complementary.

The Theological Foundations of Hiebert's "Critical Contextualization"

In a chapter which also elaborates on the original monograph, Hiebert picks up on that earlier discussion and reinforces the biblical and theological foundations of his insistence that contextualization ultimately be done in and by the church (Hiebert n.d.: 387-400). He does this by emphasizing four basic theological commitments.

First, critical contextualization is based upon the normativity of Scripture: the Bible is the fully authoritative Word of God and the rule of faith and practice. This may seem obvious but it must not be taken for granted. All contextualized practices and theologies must be measured against the standard of Scripture.

Second, Hiebert recognizes that the Holy Spirit is operative in the lives of all believers who are open to his leading. He takes the priesthood of all believers seriously.

Third, the church is a "hermeneutical community." The doctrine of the priesthood of all believers is not a license for "lone-rangerism." Rather, it is an incentive to interdependence. We see the sins of others before we see our own. For that and other reasons, we need the insights of others in the local congregation, the historical church, and the churches of other cultures.

Fourth, Hiebert sees theological discussion among evangelical theologians of various cultures increasing more and more. His theology as well as his personal aspirations lead him to believe that this will result in a growing consensus on key theological issues in contextualization and other undertakings of church and mission.

Conclusion

Going back to our story of the evangelist and D. T. Niles, we can see something of the frustration that led Niles to say in effect, "Preach and act in your own way and we will interpret the gospel for our own people." The gulf between American and Indian cultures is not bridged in three easy lessons. Niles knew that. McGavran knew it. And so do Hiebert, Nicholls, Newbigin and a host of others who are familiar with the Hindu worldview and Indian culture. That is why all of them take contextualization so seriously. At the same time, the evangelist was not to be discouraged from preaching.

Three fundamental points that stem directly from Hiebert's proposals or are complementary to them are important here.

First, extremes in contextualization are to be avoided. It is a mistake either to categorically reject or to uncritically accept the ideas and practices of any culture, including our own. It is a mistake to naively proceed as though words are set in concrete on the one hand, or completely arbitrary on the other. Both under-contextualization and over-contextualization are unwarranted.

Second, contextualization is a "community project." Christian contextualization is to be done in the context of the church. Just as the Word is to be heard, studied and obeyed in the church, so the world is best understood when analyzed in community. Depending upon the situation, missionaries and local pastors may be best equipped to instruct church members concerning basic principles of biblical interpretation. But local pastors and, especially, ordinary believers will be best equipped to provide information concerning the significance of local words, beliefs and practices.

Third, the Bible itself is the primary instrument of contextualization. I recall a Trinity conference in which contextualization discussions became complex and even a bit heated. Kenneth Kantzer rose to the occasion and reminded everyone present that in our hands we held a book that, by virtue of its supracultural *and* cultural content and character, is more appropriate, relevant, and understandable transculturally than any other book in the world. He is not alone in making that important point. In a passage dealing specifically with India but applicable to all cultures William Dyrness writes:

> I will argue . . . that it is Scripture, and not its "message," that is finally transcultural. Gospel after all means "good news" and what appears to one culture as good may not be good at all to another. For example, it does not sound like good news to a Hindu that we are "born again" in Christ, for the Hindu is trying to escape the tyrannical circle of rebirths to reach a state of final union with God. It might be that good news for this person is the final union that Christ makes possible with God—hardly a formulation that would appeal to middle-class Americans. Although it will surely relate in some way to Christ and his work,

what is transcultural is not some core truth, but Scripture—the full biblical context of Christ's work. It is this that must be allowed to strike its own spark in the light of the needs of particular cultures (Dyrness 1990: 28, emphasis mine).

We conclude this chapter and section with a "personal reflection" offered by Donald Carson rather early on in contextualization discussions as part of a response to papers on the subject by Gleason Archer and Paul Hiebert:

. . . missionary training must include substantive courses in biblical theology; for, although the study of contextualization may help the missionary free himself from the cultural accretions of his own society there is a growing danger that contextualization will be used as a new tool to pervert the gospel into something unrecognizable. Nothing will provide a better safeguard than the constant study of the Word of God (Carson 1979: 231-32).

Part III

The Place of the Bible
In Christian Ministry

6

Hans-Ruedi Weber: Confronting the World with the Gospel

World evangelization has been high on the agendas of churches and missions for over a century now. Most agree upon the urgency of evangelizing the world in the shortest possible time. But, though questions remain as to what world evangelization may mean and entail, the fundamental questions have to do with strategy and method: how best go about this essential task?

"Strategy" is really a military word. It has to do with the science or art of waging a war—the overall planning and directing of operations, the deployment of armies, making political alignments, and so on. "Method" is a less imposing word having to do with a regularized way of doing something or of going about a task.

Even a cursory review of the history of missionary and evangelistic endeavors over the last century (especially those years since World War II) is most revealing in this regard. One way of analyzing what has happened is to do so in terms of a succession of evangelistic methods that have been somehow refashioned into strategies—of one or another method being proposed as *the* best way to evangelize the world, proving itself to be *a* way of contributing to that goal, and thus yielding to another method elevated to *the* way, etc. Immediately after World War II, crusade or mass evangelism was given high priority as a means of reaching the multitudes in Japan and other countries that had suddenly reopened to missions. Then, when it became apparent that there was a wide disparity between the number of "decisions" and those being "added to the church," the search for a new strategy began in earnest. In Latin America, Kenneth Strachan had looked on as his own father led crusade after crusade. He became convinced that there had to be a better way of going about the task and subsequently became the architect of "Evangelism-in-Depth." In a short time EID campaigns were scheduled in a number of countries, EID books were published, and seminars on the EID approach became common. Then, when the weaknesses as well as the strengths of EID were made known, the emphasis shifted again. This time it shifted in the direction of personal evangelism with the use of the Four Spiritual Laws or the methods of Evangelism Explosion.

Of course, this is only part of the story. To a greater or lesser degree, the methods of the Church Growth Movement, Pocket Testament League, Every Home Crusade, Discipling a Whole Nation and other movements and organizations have been accorded similar status. The same could be said of supporting national evangelists, raising up international teams, and utilizing mass media—at one time or other all of these and still other approaches have been put forth as the most economical, effective and/or expeditious way of fulfilling the Great Commission and completing the task of world evangelization.

Let it be crystal clear that this is not written as an indictment of any of these methodologies. Of course, some are superior to others. But all have made important contributions. Some still do and will continue to do so in the future. The weakness revealed by this history is not so much that this or that evangelistic method is mistaken and misguided. The weak-

ness is that this or that method is so readily transmuted into an overall strategy for world evangelization. The weakness is not so much in the method as it is in our penchant for over-simplification and faddishness in embracing one method or partial strategy after another as an "end-all" strategy. It is that faddishness that has caused church and mission leaders in the Third World to come to the place where they view American proposals and programs with a good deal of suspicion. There is indeed one way of coming to salvation, but there are many ways of contributing to world evangelization. That is the lesson to be learned from the experience of the recent past.

Message and Method

There is another aspect of this history that must not be overlooked. It has to do, not only with method, but also with message.

When our Lord said, "And this gospel of the kingdom shall be preached in all the world for a witness to all the nations, and then the end shall come" (Matt. 24:14), he used forms of three words most intimately related to that task: *kerysso* (proclaim or announce), *martyreo* (bear witness), and *euangelizo* ("gospelize" or evangelize). (The New Testament uses still other important words such as dialogue, persuade, tell, warn, prove, and beseech as well. Back to them in a moment.)

Now if we think of the three words used in Matthew 24:14 (and elsewhere throughout the New Testament) as primary, it is of more than passing interest that various segments of the world church seem to be partial to one or another of them as a kind of umbrella word to describe the church's task in the world. Those in the Reformed tradition seem to be partial to kerygma/proclamation. Thinking more generally, those in the conciliar movement have tended to emphasize world witness. Conservatives have focused on the *euangelion* and communicating the good news of the gospel.

Similarly, if it is legitimate to think of other New Testament words such as those mentioned above as secondary or supporting words, once again most of us seem to have our preferences. Especially since the WCC meeting in New Dehli (1961) and the Second Vatican Council in Rome (1962-65), there has been an emphasis in those bodies on "dialogue with the world" and "interreligious dialogue." Subsequently and by a peculiar alchemy, witness and dialogue have been combined in such a way as to make world evangelization by ecumenists unlikely if not impossible. Let's see why this is so.

Subsequent to New Dehli and before its meeting in Uppsala (1968), the World Council of Churches established a subunit of its Program Unit on Faith and Witness called Dialogue with People of Living Faiths and Ideologies. From the beginning, WCC leadership emphasized that interfaith dialogue should be built on mutual respect for the dialogue partner and should not involve a denial of the uniqueness of Jesus Christ (Scherer 1987: 158). As practiced, however, any effort to convert others to Christ has often been categorized as "proselytization" and in some strange way interpreted as lack of respect and love for one's neighbor. History has proved that Eric J. Scharpe was essentially correct when, early on, he indicated that the theological foundations on which past polemics and "partisan controversies" rested have now been revised so that advocates of this "new form" of dialogue

> almost all assume . . . that the causes of past intolerance have to do with the doctrinal and other constructions that men have built around their central religious commitment, and seek for areas of common concern in which those constructions are transcended, penetrated or avoided (Scharpe 1974: 82).

Though independent of both Protestant and Catholic sponsorship as such, the Parliament of the World's Religions held in Chicago in 1993 was in keeping with both the purposes and spirit of ecumenical dialogue. The Parliament addressed a variety of issues facing postmodern humanity from peace to poverty to injustice. On the all-important issues having to do with humanity's eternal welfare, however, the Parliament leaders had little to offer but an insipid relativism. The program chairman, Jim Kenney, made this relativism crystal clear when he wrote:

> All in all, we could do worse than to recall the words of Swami Vivekananda: "We believe not only in universal toleration, but we accept all religions to be true." Sure, it's a dangerous proposition. But what if? And that "what if?" is the basis of interfaith dialogue. Consider this as a starting point: every religion is superior to every other by virtue of what it does best. And let's go just a bit beyond: every religion has a very secret access to the truth. *The conversation begins here!* (Kenney 1993; emphasis mine).

It is hard to imagine an approach to dialogue that is more inimical to the claims of Christ and the gospel. Nevertheless, conciliar participants in the Parliament frequently spoke of their involvement in this kind of dialogue as a meaningful form of Christian witness!

Of course, evangelicals and other conservatives have taken exception to this approach. But they are not without their own blind spots. The evangelical emphasis is not so much on witness and certainly not on dialogue. Rather it is on proclamation and the good news of the gospel (communicating the gospel, evangelizing). The problem here does not have to do with a redefinition of these biblical terms so much as it does with a truncation of the biblical task.

First, the word evangelize does indeed mean to communicate the good news of the gospel. But, though John 3:16 and similar verses encapsulate the gospel, they do not exhaust it. The biblical gospel must be set in the context of the larger biblical message. God's "good news" as in John 3:16 can only be rightly understood and truly embraced to the extent that people understand the equally biblical "bad news" concerning humankind's terrible sin and God's righteous judgment. There is little point in trying to get men and women saved before they realize that they are lost!

Secondly, evangelicals sometimes fall into the trap of thinking that if people say the "right" words or utter the "correct" prayer, that is tantamount to salvation. But, as Francis Schaeffer reminded us years ago, for more and more people today, key words related to the gospel retain less and less of their true, biblical meaning. Unless we pause to define and explain the meaning of "sin," "righteousness," "repent," "believe" and so on, we will end up speaking only to ourselves.

Thirdly, conversion tends to be understood more in terms of a "turning to," less in terms of a "turning from" when evangelicals "proclaim the good news of the gospel." The reasons for this are clear. But so are the results—namely, reversion and syncretism.

Finally, a one-sided emphasis on gospel proclamation overlooks the fact that all true communication is two-way. In the final analysis, speakers/writers communicate effectively only when they are also hearers/readers.

In short, to be biblical and effective in the attempt to evangelize a postmodern world, evangelicals should think not only in terms of proclaiming the good news of the gospel but also in terms of responding to the worldling's problems, understandings and objections. *World evangelization is not simply a matter of "communicating the gospel." It is also a matter of "confronting the world with the gospel."*

Proclamational Dialogue:
a Key Method in World Evangelization

In a scintillating but short chapter on dialogue, John R. W. Stott reminds us that the Gospels make it clear that Jesus did not retreat from two-way communication whether respondents were friends or foes. Stott writes that Jesus "seldom if ever spoke in a declamatory, take-it-or-leave-it-style. Instead, whether explicitly or implicitly, he was constantly addressing questions to his hearers' minds and consciences" (Stott 1975: 61).

The same can be said in the case of the apostle Paul.

Most of the instances where New Testament writers specifically resort to the Greek word *dialegomai* and its cognates (the noun *dialogos* does not appear in the New Testament) have to do with his ministry (cf. Acts 17:2, 17; 18:4, 19; 20:7, 9; 24:12). But in these instances a specific kind or style of dialogue is in view. Concerning this Stott goes on to say:

> Paul's dialogue was clearly a part of his proclamation and subordinate to his proclamation. Moreover, the subject of his dialogue with the world was one which he always chose himself, Jesus Christ, and its object was always conversion to Christ (Stott 1975: 63).

This being the case, Paul's dialogues with worldlings quite often involved disputation, debate and dissent. This is part of biblical dialogue as well—not a necessary part, but a part nevertheless. What is in view, after all, is not the reputation of the believer but the salvation of the unbeliever; not the embracing of the Christian but the embracing of the Christ.

To engage in biblical dialogue, then, is neither to compromise revealed truth by adding appealing notions to it nor subtracting unappealing truths from it. Its first concern is the clear communication of the whole counsel of God. Gottlob Schrenk has summed this up very well:

In the New Testament there is no instance of the classical use of *dialegomai* in the philosophical sense. In the sphere of revelation there is no question of reaching the idea through dialectic. What is at issue is the obedient and percipient acceptance of the Word spoken by God, which is not an idea, but *the comprehensive declaration of the divine will which sets all life in the light of the divine truth* (Schrenk 1964: 94; emphasis mine).

This is biblical dialogue. Elijah did not avoid it. He dialogued openly with an idolatrous queen and even the prophets of Baal. Our Lord was no stranger to it. He dialogued extensively with the scribes and Pharisees, with Nicodemus and the Samaritan woman, and even with Pilate and Herod. Paul was well acquainted with it. He dialogued in synagogues and churches, in a marketplace in Athens and a school in Ephesus, and even in the courts and prisons of Philippi, Caesarea and Rome.

The best hope for the fulfillment of the Great Commission and the evangelization of a postmodern world is that those in conciliar movement who have subscribed to an interfaith dialogue that does injustice to the biblical gospel return to Scripture and reinvigorate biblical witness. The best hope for world evangelization is that those conservative evangelicals who have tended to speak without also listening and to "pick and choose" rather than give attention to the whole counsel of God, reconsider the proclamational dialogue method of the New Testament. In every case, we must remember that it is neither the message nor the methods of the Word of God that is paramount, it is the Word of God itself. That Word is the "strategy" God uses to pull down strongholds and build his church.

Hans-Ruedi Weber in Luwuk-Banggai

For a most instructive modern illustration of the importance of biblical dialogue to world evangelization we go back in years to the 1950s and across the ocean to Indonesia.

Of a number of proponents and practitioners of biblical dialogue at home and around the world I choose to highlight the approach of the Dutch missionary-theologian Hans-Ruedi Weber. I do so because, within the ecumenical movement, Weber stands out as an unusually gifted Bible teacher and missionary who has engaged in, learned from, and instructed others in effective and biblical dialogue. Weber has repeatedly been called upon to lead Bible studies in a variety of circumstances. In some cases these stimulating studies have found their way into print (see, for example, Weber 1981 and 1989). Our focus here, however, is on his early ministry in Indonesia (see Weber 1957).

In 1952-53 Hans-Ruedi Weber was given a task that would challenge the understanding and ingenuity of even the most knowledgeable and experienced evangelist or missionary. Out of a total population of about 100,000 people living on the Luwuk peninsula and the Banggai archipelago in Central Celebes, Indonesia, at that time there was a Protestant church of about 30,000 nominal Christians. Shortly after the turn of this century, Muslim traders had begun to win a number of people in this area to Islam. At the urging of the Dutch colonial government, the Reformed state church sent a minister to the area. Over the next few years thousands were baptized.

Converts were of three types. Some were sincere. Others were baptized because they felt that they should accept the religion of their rulers. Still others, feeling that they had to accept either Islam or Christianity, opted for the latter in order to continue raising the pigs and dogs (prohibited by Islam) so necessary for their pagan sacrifices. In essence, they became Christian in order to remain pagan!

During the years that intervened from just prior to World War I to the close of World War II, the church in Lu-wuk-Banggai had grown considerably. But only ten percent of all baptized church members had received the instruction necessary to be able to participate in Communion in accordance with Reformed practice. Moreover, as many as two-thirds of the baptized Christians were nonliterate.

Weber was assigned the task of teaching these people the rudiments of biblical faith within a one-year period and without recourse to special funds or equipment. (This was to be a "Dutch treat"!) Since Weber had a great concern for evangelism, this meant not only instructing nominal Christians in biblical teachings but also in ways to bear witness to the world. To many of us that sounds like "mission impossible"—especially given the time frame of one short year. But Weber evidently did not think so. How, then, did he proceed?

Weber scheduled five-day Bible courses in a central village of each of seven church districts. Churches sent a few members to the Bible study course who would be able to return to their churches and teach others.

The format of the five-day Bible course for Luwuk-Banggai church representatives was at once simple and profound. By way of introduction, the importance of the Bible in the life of the Christian and the congregation was stressed. The first evening, the "travel route" to be taken through the Bible was sketched: creation to the Kingdom of God in the book of Revelation including the Fall, the covenants with Israel, the church, and the Second Coming, with Christ at the center of the whole. Later, rough drawings were added to illustrate and symbolize biblical events and teachings.

The four succeeding days highlighted Genesis 3:1-19, Exodus 19:1-6, Luke 2:8-14, and Acts 1:6-11. Each day began with worship, a reading of the Scripture passage of the day, and prayer for guidance. Then the assigned passage was studied in small groups, making sure that it was linked with preceding studies. Following this study each group reported its findings and a summary was drawn up.

Afternoons were spent in discussing community life, the meaning of baptism and Communion, the importance of evangelism, and similarly important topics. Evenings were spent in discussing the role of Christians in the contexts of a tribal community, modern Islam, and the larger world.

All led up to the last evening which was devoted to bearing witness to the people of the village in which the Bible course was held. Since outreach is the special focus of this chapter, we will take a closer look at the ways in which Weber and his fellow Christians communicated the gospel to their pagan neighbors in Luwuk-Banggai.

Confronting the People of
Luwuk-Banggai with the Gospel

Weber claims that the climax of the five-day course of Bible study invariably came on the last evening (Weber 1957: 4). The theme of the final study on Acts 1:6-11 was "Ye shall be my witnesses," so participants immediately began to witness together. They began by inviting the entire village—believers and unbelievers—to a community gathering. In anticipation of community witness, some short dramas and vignettes had been prepared during the course of study. Now on this final night several of these were presented to the villagers. For example, in order to show how people worshipped God in Old Testament times, the Jerusalem temple was "reconstructed" out of tables and seats, and its porches out of the leaves of the coconut-palm. Then Psalm 24 or Psalm 100 was recited antiphonally by "High Priest" and "Levite," and a chorus of men and women. From the New Testament, some of the parables of Jesus were mimed; the audience was asked to guess what the parable was; the relevant Bible passage was read; and a biblical exposition and challenge was given. All of this was set within the framework of certain Christian hymns that had been learned during the course of study.

Following a time for tea and rice-cakes, and of fare-wells and thank-you speeches, the evening ended with Christian worship. The first evening of the Bible course had featured a reading of Genesis 1 concerning the creation of heaven and earth. Now, in the company of all, the last evening pointed to the consummation of the drama of salvation and featured a reading of Revelation 21 with its vision of a recreated world and a kingdom of peace.

Growing out of his experiences on these occasions, Weber conducted an "experiment." During his travels Weber came to Taulan, a small island with but one village. Some of the inhabitants had become believers, but many had not. The Christians invited the entire village to come together. Weber indicates that almost all accepted the invitation. "There," he writes, "the entire village assembled—animals and humans, Christians and non-Christians, babies in arms and old men (among them the heathen priest)—all of them illiterate" (Weber 1957: 6). Using a few planks as a blackboard for his simple drawings, Weber began with the story of creation from the book of Genesis, drawing as he spoke. Then the heathen priest was asked to relate the story of creation as reported in the legends of the people. The two stories were compared. Next the story of the Fall in Genesis was compared and contrasted with legends of the origin of evil as handed down from generation to generation in Taulan.

And so the dialogue continued until the gathering recessed for a late lunch. Then in the afternoon everyone reassembled and the dialogue was continued.

Encouraged by the results of the Taulan "experiment," this method was used in other villages. Everywhere Weber's approach met with an enthusiastic response. Later, in Java and Bali, he added comparisons of Christian symbols with non-Christian symbols such as the Buddhist zoetrope, the Taoist sign, and the Communist hammer and sickle. Over several months Weber perfected his evangelistic method in a way that made the gospel meaningful to literates and nonliterates alike.

Weber insists that, though he was the teacher, he became a pupil in order to communicate with the people of Luwuk-Banggai. As a pupil he says that he learned several important lessons:

1) It is a mistake to treat nonliterates as children and merely tell Bible stories. All must be set in a complete redemptive history—creation and eschatology; the history of Israel, of the church, and of the Christian mission; and Christ the center of it all. In other words, Jesus must not be "de-Judaized" lest he be "de-historicized" and Christianity be put in the framework of the mythological.

2) Once the mythological framework has been shattered, the classification and integrating character of so-called "primitive thinking" can be seen as a great gift. The people of Luwuk-Banggai and others like them are able to cope with any event because it can be absorbed in their myth. As Christians they can cope to the extent that they know the beginning, center and end of history.

3) Most important, according to Weber, is the fact that he learned about a "new Bible." Concerning this he writes:

> The most exciting discovery of that time, however, was a new Bible: the Bible as the story and oral tradition of God's great acts, the Bible as God's picturebook, the Bible pointing to the symbols by which God both conceals and reveals himself (Weber 1989: 4).

Future Dialogue with the World

Weber doesn't say a lot about dialogue as such. His emphasis is on the importance of the Bible in evangelizing and instructing even nonliterates. But whether he analyzes biblical dialogue or not, and whether one agrees with Weber in other matters or not, it is not difficult to see the advantages of his dialogical method. At that point, the vast majority of both ecumenists and evangelicals alike would benefit from a re-education. In post-Christian First and Second Worlds as well as what some term a pre-Christian Third World, it is essential that unbelievers understand the Christian faith as a unique alternative—not just another expression of, or adjunct to, or even fulfillment of, their present system of belief or unbelief. There is no better way to meet that need for understanding and encouraging true conversion than by practicing biblical dialogue of the kind demonstrated by Hans-Ruedi Weber. That he practiced it in the context of untutored and often nonliterate animists is in itself instructive. That he did it by a clear and consistent usage of the main outlines of the biblical story is even more so.

Of course, we could point to many other contemporaries who, in very different circumstances, have resorted to this form of communication and with good effect—John Stott in his dialogue with the liberal English church historian David L. Edwards; Josh McDowell and Norman Geisler in their dialogues with skeptics and atheists in American universities; Walter Kaiser, Gleason Archer and others in their dialogues with prominent American Jewish scholars; Phil Parshall and Don Rickards in their dialogues with Muslim leaders in the Philippines and the Middle East. We need to do a much better job of training future leaders who will be capable and comfortable in dialogues of this sort.

But in looking to these who have excelled in gaining knowledge and honing their communication skills over the years, we should not lose sight of the fact that no matter who we are and whatever our status, two-way dialogical communication remains as one of the most effective communication modes available to us in a pluralistic and relativistic world. All of us can afford to give much more attention to questions that worldlings are asking. And when we do not know what they believe, we ourselves can ask. And, if we know the Scriptures, we like Weber can counter, "That's interesting, but in his Word God has purposed and planned . . . ."

Conclusion

With the foregoing in mind, we conclude with some lessons gleaned from a passage often used to illustrate the method of the apostle Paul—Acts 17:16-34. Luke's Spirit-inspired summary of Paul's message at the meeting of the Areopagus in Athens makes it clear that it must have been a classic "sermon." Indeed, the text appears not only in the Bible but even today can be found engraved on a bronze plate on the side of Mars Hill. Intrigued with Paul's approach, various commentators have studied it in order to obtain clues for effective communication of the gospel to adherents of non-Christian religions and philosophies. In so doing, they have noted certain clues that are critical to future dialogue. Consider some of them.

First, dialogue should communicate objective truth—what God has done in history and the meaning God himself has assigned to the things he has done. In other times and places Paul testified as to what God had done for, in and through Saul of Tarsus. But it does not seem that Paul often used his personal experience as a basis for persuading others. In David Wells's words, he proclaimed not the experience of Christ, but the Christ of experience (Wells 1991: 276). In Athens as elsewhere he proclaimed *public* truth—the acts and pronouncements of the Creator God and Lord of history (vss. 24, 26-27, 30-31).

Second, dialogue should be based on knowledge and highlight comparisons and contrasts with local belief systems. Though numerous commentators have noted the "common ground" approach implicit in Paul's references to an altar to the "unknown god" and an Athenian poet, Paul actually gave more attention to the stark contrast between Athenian idols and worship on the one hand and the true God and true worship on the other (vss. 24-25, 29-30). Since "commonalities," "redemptive analogies" and the like draw upon world systems antagonistic to the gospel, they are always tenuous at best. Contrasts are more definitive, and often more convincing and compelling at the same time.

Third, dialogue should not disregard those aspects of the gospel that might be thought of as offensive or objectionable. Paul took note of the "ignorance" of his hearers (vs. 30). He emphasized not Christ's cross and its meaning but Christ's resurrection and its significance (vss. 31-32). He insisted that Christ will judge the world in justice (vs. 31). Of course, Luke's summary is not complete. And we know from other passages that the cross and forgiveness were intrinsic to Paul's message. But in a time when people are offered forgiveness when they do not know what sin is, and salvation before they know what they need to be saved from, Paul's approach is especially instructive.

Fourth, dialogue is intrinsic to effective communication of the gospel in a pluralistic world. It should be noticed that the so-called Athenian discourse grew out of dialogical conversations in the synagogue and marketplace (vs. 17). Also that the discourse itself, if monological in form, was dialogical in method. It was a response to inquiries about this "new teaching" and these "strange ideas," (vss. 19-20) and to what Athenians were really thinking and doing. Somehow and some way, Christian communicators of the future will have to rethink and reframe their approach to the world and prepare themselves for a more studied and sustained communication of Christian truth.

Fifth, dialogists must be willing to be lightly esteemed and be prepared for seeming failure. In Athens some of the citizenry called Paul a "babbler" (a *spermalogos* or "seed picker," vs. 18). When he finished his message at the Areopagus some sneered, some procrastinated, and only a few believed (vss. 32-34). When Paul departed for Corinth to begin another dialogue, this time with Jews and Greeks in a synagogue (Acts 18:4), there is nothing to indicate that he had made much of an impact on Athens. According to Luke's modest reckoning, Dionysius, Damaris, and a few other believers were left behind. That's about it. Purveyors of instant success would find little to crow about here. Biblical dialogue with the world is not always up-lifting and encouraging as far as numbers go. But, questions and objections having been dealt with as a part of the decision process, results are often deeper and more lasting. It might have been so even in Athens because, long after some of the churches identified in the New Testament are no longer heard from, history records that Athens was the home of a thriving church with outstanding leaders.

Historians often take note of the fact that, of all the in-tervening periods of history, our times are most like the Med-iterranean world of the first century. Reframed in accordance with first-century guidelines, might it not be that future dia-logue with our world will yield results similar to those achieved by the first-century church?

7

Trevor McIlwain:
Confirming Believers
in the Christian Faith

Talk to almost any pastor or missionary about problems faced in local congregations at home or abroad. In all likelihood one problem will have to do with getting seekers and new converts into the fellowship of the local church. Another will likely have to do with transforming church attenders into involved, mature members of the congregation.

Our emphasis and efforts on "follow-up" have perhaps helped to narrow the gap between mass evangelism and the local church but have not closed it by any means.

Our endeavors to make the worship service appealing and meaningful have in many cases resulted in increased attendance on Sunday mornings but have not necessarily increased membership and enhanced spiritual growth.

Our concentration on discipleship has enabled some believers to grow in the faith and go out in witness, but all too often the majority of Christians still sit on the sidelines preoccupied with their personal questions and difficulties.

Our group Bible studies certainly have had a positive

impact, but all too often they neglect basic principles of biblical interpretation and are detached from the program of the local church.

In spite of these and still other attempts to make real believers out of sincere seekers, mature saints out of nominal Christians, and New Testament churches out of ordinary congregations, there is still much room for improvement. There always will be, but that does not justify the staus quo. Our present problems need attention. They have to do, not so much with what we have done, but with what we have failed to do. Not so much with our "sins" of commission, as with our "sins" of omission.

The Scope of the Great Commission

When our Lord gave the Great Commission, he claimed all authority in heaven and earth and then commanded his followers to go into all the world and make disciples by baptizing and teaching all that he commanded (Matt. 28:18-20). In one sense, of course, Muslims are correct in noting that Jesus never married a wife, fathered children, ran a business, or commanded an army. In another sense, they are dead wrong. He has a bride, many children, a going business, an everlasting kingdom and an army that is advancing around the world. All of that because of who he was, what he did, and what he commanded his followers to do. Since the obedience of his followers has not been total, however, progress has come by fits and starts. The command itself was both extensive and intensive. Anything approaching full obedience would have resulted in a very different situation both in the world and in the church itself.

Only very gradually and after considerable controversy did the churches that came out of the Reformation reach a general consensus that the Great Commission responsibility extends to all believers and all churches. And only after that consensus was reached did they begin to concentrate on "all the world" and "all nations." For a century now, much thought has been given to the scope of the field—who needs to be reached, where they are located, and how to reach them in the shortest possible time.

Today's Christians are beneficiaries of those who in the more distant past have thought deeply about who bears the responsibility and shares the privilege of obedience to the Great Commission. We are also beneficiaries of those who, in more recent days, have given serious consideration to ways of thinking about the world—about people groups and their characteristics, numbers and locations. *Now it is incumbent upon us to give more serious consideration to the fact that the Great Commission is intensive as well as extensive, that what is to be done is as comprehensive as who is to do it and and to whom it is to be done.*

Picking up the thread of the previous chapter, we now take note of three facts. First, the most complete statement of the Great Commission is found in Matthew 28:16-20. Other statements are equally important in that they too are given by the Christ who possesses all authority. But on the basis of a hermeneutical principle that less clear and comprehensive statements are to be understood in the light of those that are more so, the Matthean version becomes especially important.

Second, the sole imperative and central activity in the Commission as recorded in Matthew 28 is to "make disciples." "Go" could be translated "going" or "as you go," but takes any imperatival force it may have from the main verb. "Baptizing" and "teaching" are also participles but clearly do take the imperatival force from the main verb. In fact, the grammatical construction would indicate that this is the way disciples are to be made. But the end product is to be disciples—not "decisions" or "converts" or "believers" or "acceptors," but "disciples." It goes without saying that decision-making, conversion, belief, and acceptance are all involved, but the objective of the Great Commission is that we make disciples (followers, adherents, learners, students) of the Lord Jesus. Discipleship is not for a "select" few whom we single out; it is for all the "elect" of God in Christ!

Third, our Lord uses the word "all" three times in the Great Commission—*all* authority, *all* nations or peoples, and *all* he commanded. Why is it that we emphasize all authority and all nations, but when it comes to preaching and teaching we settle for as little of what Christ has commanded as possible? Jesus himself emphasized the whole of Scripture. His teaching was replete with references to the Old Testament. He said, "You search the Scriptures, because you think that in them you have eternal life; and it is these that bear witness of Me" (John 5:39). His promise of the Spirit secured the authority of the New Testament. To the apostles he said:

> But when He, the Spirit of truth, comes, He will guide you into all the truth; for He will not speak of His own initiative, but whatever He hears, He will speak; and He will disclose to you what is to come. He shall glorify Me; for He shall take of Mine, and shall disclose it to you (John 16:13-14).

Of course, we cannot communicate the whole of Scripture in one sitting. In that sense we will have to be selective. But we should never be selective to the exclusion of the whole or unpalatable parts of the whole. We should never divorce a part of the gospel from the whole of it. Rather, the part that we select and the way that we treat it should direct hearers to the whole of the gospel, to the larger story of Scripture. John Nevius wisely counseled his missionary colleagues to the effect that, when they preached to Chinese who were hearing the Christian message for the first time, unless they themselves could stay on to instruct converts in the faith, they should exhort hearers to accept those who would come later with the teaching of Jesus.

When we preach a very select gospel to unbelievers and

reserve complete teaching for a very select group of believers, we create great gaps between decisions and discipleship, between the majority and the mature. Moreover, we do injustice to our mandate.

The Nature of the Church

Our Lord promised that he would build his church and that the gates of Hades would not overpower it (Matt. 16:18). In one sense, the Lord Jesus did not build anything. In another sense, it has been his purpose and plan to build the church from the beginning. Unless we keep this latter truth in mind, we lose divine focus and concentrate on building our school or our organization or our program or even "our" church. For a while after the middle of this century churches and especially missions tended to lose focus. However, church growth and then church planting advocates caused us to re-focus on the necessity of growing local congregations around the world. However, a renewed appreciation for the *importance* of the local church has not always resulted in a better understanding of the *nature* of the local church.

There are various ways of inquiring into the true nature of the church and its significance for churches today. First and foremost we should engage in a study of ecclesiology, the theology of the church in Scripture. This is especially important because many who serve as pastors and missionaries currently have been converted and nurtured in parachurch organizations but only loosely tied to local congregations. Missiologists especially have noted that many missionary volunteers who pass muster when it comes to Christology and soteriology, flounder and even fail on the field because of their neglect of ecclesiology. Secondly, we need to reexamine the churches of the New Testament to see where they succeeded, where they failed, and how they were instructed by the apostles. The church of Pentecost (Acts 2:41-47) has been most often held up as a model of the kind of church a Spirit-led church should be. Some other churches we do well to emulate are those in Antioch, Ephesus, Philippi and Thessalonica. But, of course, no local congregation is perfect and so we have much to learn from the shortcomings of these churches and especially of churches such as those in Corinth and the churches in Asia addressed by John in Revelation 2 and 3.

Thirdly, it is helpful to examine the metaphors used to describe the church in the New Testament. A study of the church as building, bride, body, household, etc., is both exciting and instructive.

Fourthly, descriptions of New Testament church life and witness should be undertaken as well. For example, when we compare worship, fellowship and prayer in the New Testament with our understandings and practices today, we find similarities to be sure. But we also find glaring differences.

Of course, the above is sketchy at best. But I mention it because, however New Testament ecclesiology is approached, its study will reveal that one of the greatest weaknesses of the contemporary church has to do with a proper use and knowledge of the Bible itself. After the baptism of about "three thousand souls" on Pentecost, the very first thing Luke mentions is that they "were continually devoting themselves to the apostles' teaching" (Acts 2:41). When Paul writes of the duty of the "person-gifts" of the risen Christ to his church (i.e., apostles, prophets, evangelists and pastor-teachers), he indicates that they should equip the saints for the work of service, the building of the body and the unity of the faith (Eph. 4:11-12). When he exhorts Ephesian believers to be prepared for spiritual warfare, he puts special emphasis on the shield of faith and the sword of the Spirit, the Word of God (Eph. 6:16-17). When the writer of Hebrews wants to teach Jewish congregations about the priesthood of Christ, he notes their inability to digest "solid food" and scolds them for being spiritual babies when they ought to be teachers (Heb. 5:12).

What about our churches today? It is said that the average home in the United States has at least four or five Bibles. Most churches have Bibles in every pew. Many congregations have confirmation classes and most have Sunday Schools. Christian bookstores stock a variety of modern Bible translations. Home Bible studies abound. Nevertheless, one of the most astounding commentaries frequently heard is that when it comes to the Scriptures, American laypeople today are less well informed than their forebears and even than some nonliterate Christians in the Two-Thirds world! Upon becoming acquainted with the churches of our country, the Lutheran theologian Harry Wendt became so appalled with what he identified as biblical illiteracy (Lutheran confirmation notwithstanding) that he risked all his resources in developing the Divine Drama materials and establishing Crossways International (now headquartered in Minneapolis). It is interesting that, though these studies have been developed at three graded levels, none is for children. Wendt's philosophy is that it is the duty of adults to teach children but that, before they are equipped to teach, they will first have to learn themselves.

Equally arresting is the recent history of New Tribes Mission on which we will expand in a moment. After developing a Bible study approach called Firm Foundations designed to confirm Palawano believers in the Christian faith and discovering that the Holy Spirit had used the Word of God to mature them in a remarkable way, Trevor McIlwain was returned to the States and given the task of preparing materials for some 3,000 New Tribes missionaries working on seventeen fields around the world. One of the fascinating aspects of this history is that as American Christians and churches have become aware of Firm Foundations materials and their effectiveness in other lands, there has been a dramatic demand for the same study materials right here at home. "Bread" sent across the waters is washing back upon our shores to sustain the senders!

Trevor McIlwain and the
Palawano Churches of the Philippines

Currently, Trevor McIlwain is the International Co-ordinator for Church Planting and Evangelism with New Tribes Mission. He is also author of the multi-volume series *Building on Firm Foundations*. The version being used among English-speaking people begins with a volume entitled *Foundations: Creation to Christ*, but translations are also available or in progress in Russian, Spanish, Portuguese, Rumanian (for their public school system), Chinese and many tribal languages.

In 1965 the Trevor McIlwains left their native Australia for the Philippines. They were to take up work among the Pa-lawano tribespeople living on the island of Palawan in the southwestern region of that country. A work had been estab-lished among the Palawanos shortly after the end of World War II and as many as forty small scattered churches already ex-isted. However, the churches were beset with most of the prob-lems that afflicted larger Palowano society—divorce and re-marriage, drunkenness, and much else. More than that, there seemed to be widespread misunderstanding of what it really means to be a Christian. In spite of the best efforts of the mis-sionaries to instruct and exhort believers, many of them were caught in a cycle of repenting of their evil ways, functioning outwardly as Christians for a while, falling back into the old ways, being challenged by missionaries and pastors, being "re-vived," and starting the cycle all over again.

To understand this state of affairs, one must be aware of at least two factors that contributed to it. First, for decades the Palawanos had been a downtrodden and afflicted people. Long years before many had been murdered and maimed by ma-rauding Moros (Muslim sea warriors). Then came settlers who emigrated from surrounding islands and forced them from their homes back into inhospitable foothills and mountains. But the worst was still to come. The Japanese invasion inaugurated a period of rape, devastation and death previously unknown. Finally, along with the rest of the Philippines, Palawan was liberated by the "Amerikans." The liberators took pride in protecting their "little Palawano brothers," but their withdrawal once again left tribespeople to fend for themselves. Then an American missionary arrived who displayed a great love and concern for them. Something of a "people movement" ensued. Several thousand Palawanos professed conversion, were baptized and organized into local churches. As one Palawano put it, "We would have done anything for that first missionary. If he had asked us to cut our fingers off, we would have gladly done it for him" (McIlwain 1987: 12). That being the case, one can appreciate the fact that conversions stemmed from very mixed motives.

Second, it must be understood that succeeding missionaries did everything they knew how to instruct Palawano church members as to the true meaning of conversion and baptism, and what it meant to live the Christian life. Even if one could fault the pioneer missionary for inadequate instruction before baptizing converts and organizing churches—difficult to do given the openness of the people and the scarcity of workers—it certainly would be impossible to criticize successors because they did what the vast majority of dedicated missionaries would do in similar circumstances! In fact, initially Trevor McIlwain himself employed what we might call "standard methodology" in order to correct the situation.

Applying Instructional "Correctives"

When the McIlwains took up residence among the Palawanos in the mid-sixties he was given special responsibility for instructing church members and elders from the Scriptures in such a way as to bring them to Christian maturity. He began by traveling among the churches and questioning believers concerning their understanding of God and his plan of salvation: "What must one do to be saved?" "What if a person believes but is not baptized or does not attend church regularly, is that person saved?" and, "What if one truly trusts Christ but gets drunk or commits adultery. Could he be saved?" Answers to questions such as these revealed that Palawano Christians really did not understand biblical doctrine and based their salvation on a mixture of faith and works.

After some months, another approach was introduced, especially with church leaders. Realizing that Palawanos would always agree with a teacher and that they would have to take a stand against teachers of false cults who were beginning to arrive in increasing numbers, McIlwain began teaching biblical truth concerning salvation and then contradicting that truth by teaching error. At first this confused his hearers but, gradually, church leaders learned to think for themselves and discern the difference between truth and error.

Over a period of time, many Palawanos came to a better understanding of the cardinal doctrine of justification by faith. Many who had merely professed Christ were truly saved and many more received assurance of salvation. While this was indeed gratifying to the missionaries, the task of bringing so many scattered "babes in Christ" to spiritual maturity still seemed staggering. So McIlwain abandoned his itinerant ministry, settled in the middle of six small churches, and began to teach the Scripture topically and expositionally, verse by verse.

Since the churches were attended by true believers, mere professors and some unbelievers, McIlwain singled out the Gospel of John for intensive study. Initially there was considerable enthusiasm for the study. However, problems cropped up almost from the start:

John 1:1—"In the beginning was the Word." The Palawanos did not understand the meaning of "beginning" or "Word." They had not understood that Jesus was with the Father before the beginning.

John 1:3—"All things were made by him." They had not understood that "God" in the first chapter of Genesis included Jesus.

John 1:11—"He came unto his own." Without knowing about Abraham, Israel and early promises of a Messiah this verse had little meaning for Palawano people.

Similar problems surfaced when McIlwain selected the book of Romans for verse-by-verse expositional study.

Whether approached topically or textually, expositional teaching of John, Romans and other New Testament books resulted in frustration as time and time again the teacher was forced to go back to the Old Testament in order to explain the New. Clearly there had to be a better way.

A "New View" of the "Old Book"

McIlwain recounts how he began to awaken to the fact that the Bible needed to be considered as a whole,

> as God's complete unified message to all mankind. I realized the Old Testament is not a compilation of interesting stories to be used only as types and illustrations of New Testament truth. The Old Testament is the logical introduction, foundation, and authority for the story of Christ recorded in the New Testament. The Old Testament is by far the most important source of interpretive background material for the historical accounts of the New Testament. Just as God has given us two lips and both are necessary for clear verbal [oral—ed.] communication, even so both Old and New Testaments are indispensable for the communication of God's complete message to the world (McIlwain 1987: 67-68).

This "new view" of the Bible entailed a number of concepts which have been fleshed out in McIlwain's subsequent works:

1) The entire Bible centers in God's message con-

cerning his Son, Jesus Christ. It is "His-story" from the first verse in Genesis to the last verse in Revelation. This means, for example, that though missionaries should learn all they can about the culture, folklore and belief system of the people, it is still more important to understand the prophecies, types and figures of the Old Testament itself. For example, the key both to understanding the biblical message of Christ and communicating that message to the people is not the discovery of redemptive analogies in the culture but the disclosure of redemptive analogies in the Old Testament.

2) Not only the message, but also the literary styles and forms of Scripture, are essential to proper understanding and effective instruction. In giving us the Bible, God as the Supreme Teacher has provided us with the best ways to captivate human imagination and effect clear communication. The church errs when it ignores the methods of presentation employed by the divine Author of Scripture and completely reorganizes biblical subject matter and employs its own methods of instruction.

3) The Bible is the historical record of God's acts. God has not only spoken, he has acted and interacted with people— real people over a long period of time and representing a variety of cultures. Moreover, he has acted on behalf of his chosen people in special ways. Therefore, people from any culture and time can identify with the biblical record. It is especially important that God's people take note of that identification.

4) The method of the apostles underscores the importance of these principles. They emphasized the words and works of God in history. Beginning with Peter on Pentecost and proceeding through the book of Acts and the epistles, it is clear that the apostolic method was to ground the gospel in history, especially that of the Old Testament. Not to emulate them in this regard is tantamount to erecting a building without a foundation.

In short, then, McIlwain became convinced that biblical theology—not just theology that is biblical—is foundational both to communicating the gospel to unbelievers and to confirming the church in the Christian faith. To neglect biblical theology is to invite misunderstanding, syncretism and immaturity.

The Chronological Teaching Approach

Based upon the foregoing experiences and principles, the "Chronological Teaching Approach" was developed. Though it allows for topical teaching aimed at correcting specific errors in doctrine and practice, it highlights biblical theology, the chronology of Scripture, and narrative communication. The entire course of study is divided into four phases as in Figure 6 (adapted from McIlwain 1981: 12a-12-c and 1987: 131 by Richard L. Langston).

As a review of the outline on page 117 will reveal, the first four phases of the Chronological Teaching materials are panoramic and cover the entire Bible in a relatively short period of time. Phase I emphasizes salvation and targets unbelievers, mixed groups (believers and unbelievers) and new believers. It is predicated on the conviction that saving faith—faith that bases salvation on Christ and his finished work alone—involves an understanding of God and his dealings with humankind in history. It therefore begins with creation in Genesis and ends with the ascension in the book of Acts. It emphasizes the nature of God, the meaning of sin, and God's solution (Jesus Christ) as revealed in the historical events and teachings of the whole Bible. For example, the giving of, and response to, the Law is emphasized because "through the law we become conscious of sin" (Rom. 3:20). The Old Testament promises of a Messiah and redemptive types are emphasized because they are fulfilled in Christ. The chronology of the Scriptures becomes important because it reveals the unfolding of God's redemptive plan. And so on. Taught in this way, *unbelievers* better understand what is involved in turning from false faith or no faith to saving faith in the Lord Jesus. Taught

OLD TESTAMENT	GOSPELS	ACTS	EPISTLES

<--ascension of Christ

PHASE 1 Unbelievers and/or Believers
Simple historical story from Genesis to ascension of Christ
Law   Law and the Gospel
Nature and character of God, man, Satan, and sin   God's requirements fulfilled in Jesus
Emphasis: Salvation

PHASE 2 New Believers
Review of Phase 1 material + additional O.T. stories to lay the foundation for Acts and the Epistles
Emphases: 1. Security of the Believer and the Holy Spirit
2. Christ's fulfillment of O.T. prophecies about the redeemer

PHASE 3 New Believers
Simple exposition of basic parts of Acts and historical background of Epistles
Story after the ascension and fulfillment of promises about the Holy Spirit

PHASE 4 New Believers
Simple exposition of basic portions of the Epistles
Function of NT Church and the Walk of the Believer

PHASE 5 Maturing Believers
O.T. portions concerning sanctification   Gospel portions re:
of God's servants and Israel   Training of disciples
Emphasis: Sanctification   thru fellowship with Jesus

PHASE 6 Maturing Believers
Verse-by-verse Teaching
Holy Spirit's guidance, training, and sanctifying work in Early Church and Paul's life

PHASE 7 Maturing Believers
Expositional Teaching
The Church and the Walk of the Believer

in this way, whether in mixed groups or by themselves, *believers* better understand what is involved in instructing unbelievers concerning God's plan of salvation and therefore are enabled to continue the process on their own!

Phase II also focuses on the fulfillment of the promises and types of the Old Testament in the person and work of the Redeemer as satisfying the requirements of a righteous and holy God. Unlike Phase I, however, the emphasis here is more on the security of the believer rather than on salvation per se. Phase II also deals with the person and work of the Holy Spirit as revealed in the Old Testament and the gospels.

Phase III provides an introduction to the book of Acts with its story of the ministry of the apostles, the development of the early church, and the geographical spread of Christianity from Jerusalem and its environs to Rome itself. Just as the Old Testament and the gospels provide a foundation for an understanding of the New Testament, so the book of Acts provides the background for understanding the epistles.

Phase IV is also directed at new believers and highlights the central portions of the remaining books of the New Testament with special attention being given to the functioning of the church and the walk of the believer.

Finally, Phases I, VI and VII are for "maturing believers." They emphasize, in order, sanctification as taught from Genesis to the ascension, an in-depth study of Acts and how the Holy Spirit worked in the early experiences of the church and in the life and ministry of Paul, and the remainder of the New Testament with a more in-depth study of what we might call Christian discipline in the church and the believer.

Conclusion

As might be expected, McIlwain's work is not without its critics. From the perspective of some it is too intensive and too extensive. Others feel that, though McIlwain encourages an understanding of culture, the approach is not sufficiently culture-sensitive. Still others can be expected to take exception to its doctrinal stance, reflecting as it does the New Tribes Mission statement of faith.

Nevertheless, I readily admit to a special appreciation for McIlwain's work. Shortly after establishing the New Tribes Mission in 1942, founder Paul Fleming spoke in chapel at my seminary. He was indeed a man of vision and passion, but he greatly oversimplified the task of world evangelization, leaving the strong impression that the message of John 3:16 is sufficient for its completion and that anyone, with or without special gifts, abilities and training, can communicate John 3:16. It did not require an extended time on the mission field to realize that that simply is not the case. It is especially significant that now, after fifty years, New Tribes Mission supplies a much needed corrective.

There is yet another reason for my appreciation. At one stage of my ministry in Japan, I had the unique opportunity to initiate a Bible study for as many as one hundred of Japan's outstanding technologists. Like McIlwain I chose to begin with the Gospel of John. Like him I found that their lack of background in the Scriptures rendered the study quite incomprehensible to all but a few of my students. Unlike him, I did not have the opportunity to make a new start. Some good came out of that study, but in more recent years it has occurred to me that something similar to McIlwain's model would have been much more appropriate and, perhaps, more productive as well.

Finally, I trust that it will not escape the notice of my readers that, both in the approach of Weber and that of McIlwain, the evangelism of unbelievers and the confirmation of believers are closely allied. After all, the same Holy Spirit uses the same Divine Word to accomplish both ministries. And both are aspects of one Great Commission.

8

Timothy M. Warner:
Counseling Christians
Concerning Spiritual Warfare

"Please help me!" "Please, help . . . !" "Please . . . !" In one way or another more people seem to be crying out for help than ever before. The decade of the 1980s has been referred to as the "Decade of Greed." Some predict that the 1990s will ultimately be known as the "Decade of Need." It's not just people of the world who are crying out for help, but people of the church as well. It's not just people of the church, but people of missions. And it's not just the laity but also Christian leaders at home and abroad.

Recently, the chairman of the board of elders of an evangelical church on the West Coast announced that the pastor's time and energy were being eaten up with counseling. Henceforth the pastor would be available for no more than two counseling sessions with any parishioner. After that the parishioner would be referred to a professional Christian counselor.

A year or two ago, a faculty colleague who continually ministers in a variety of churches across the country remarked that in his lifetime he had never seen so many pastor couples who were experiencing deep distress of one kind or another, either in relation to their congregations or in relation to each other and their children.

Presenting the results of his research on missionary attrition in 1992, John G. Kayser referred to one study after another that reported unusually high rates of stress and dropouts among overseas missionaries (Kayser 1992).

All of this comes at a time when there are more professional psychologists and counselors, more psychology courses and seminars, more books on self-help and self-improvement than ever before—not just in the larger society but in the church as well. And, ironically, we export both our problems and our solutions to churches and Christians overseas as part of the missionary enterprise. Go to Central and South America, for example, and you will discover numerous titles on courtship, marriage, childrearing, stress, management, etc., on the shelves of Christian bookstores. The majority of them are translations of North American publications that have questionable value in cultures as different as those north and south of the Mexican border.

It adds up to a rather dismal picture. But there is a bright side as well. Remember? How often have we heard a message that says:

> Whatever your question, there is an answer. Whatever your problem, there is a solution. We have not been promised that there will be no struggle, no difficulties, no temptations, no pain. But we have been promised strength for each day and a way through our problems.

Who has promised? God. Where is the promise? In the Scriptures. A former colleague and specialist in homiletics and preaching, Lloyd Perry, used to tell his pastoral students that if they would preach the Word faithfully and correctly they would not need to spend so much time in counseling their parishioners! Let's keep that in mind as we take a brief look backward to see how it is that we have arrived "where we are" before we look at the Book!

Some Developments in Pastoral Theology, Psychology and Counseling

In a historical overview, James Lapsley says that, although the term "pastoral theology" came into use in the middle of the eighteenth century, significant developments did not come until the nineteenth and especially the twentieth centuries (Lapsley 1969: 32). Friedrich Schleiermacher wrote on the subject in the nineteenth century, but he emphasized the theological nature of the discipline. The scientific aspect was first emphasized in the work of the Englishman Clement F. Rogers and the American Anton T. Boisen early in this century. Through the work of the latter the Clinical Pastoral Education (CPE) movement was born.

During the 1930s and 1940s, evangelical schools entertained a general distrust of psychology in general and the CPE movement in particular (cf. Collins 1980: 32-34). Experience seemed to take precedence over Scripture; the notions of psychology were borrowed too uncritically; and little attention was given to conservative theology. After World War II, however, conservatives like Clyde Narramore and Henry Brandt demonstrated that the Bible can be both believed and used by psychologists/counselors. Gradually, resistance broke down. Schools introduced courses and then whole departments of pastoral psychology and counseling. Specialists in pastoral counseling and professional psychologists, and then popularizers, arrived on the scene in increasing numbers. Finally, departments and even schools of psychology and counseling (note the omission of "pastoral") were established in order to train, not only or primarily pastors, but psychologists and counselors who would then be certified by government agencies.

While this evolution was going on in Christian churches

and schools, psychology and counseling theories and practices themselves were in the process of change. Perhaps the simplest way of summarizing what was happening is to resort to the familiar understanding according to which Western psychology has been described in terms of three or four "forces" or forceful trends.

Early on psychology was more or less dominated by the so-called "first-force" psychoanalytic theories associated with Sigmund Freud and his younger colleague, Carl Jung. Then came "second-force" behaviorism associated with the classical conditioning theories of Ivan Pavlov and Joseph Wolpe, and midway through this century, complemented by the mental-conditioning approach of B. F. Skinner.

Already developing by that time, however, was a humanistic psychology (the "third force") that would eclipse both Freudian and Pavlovian models of personality and behavior development and change. Most influential in those early days was the work of Abraham Maslow but soon to be added was the influence of people like Carl Rogers and Rollo May. I recall how, about 1950, one of my university professors returned from a conference held, as I remember, in the University of Nebraska. His report came like a breath of fresh air to those of us who had grown weary of watching rats and mice running around in mazes. His summary report went something like this:

> Maslow said that there is something uniquely different about humans. If you want to know why a rat or orangutan does this or that you have to carry out all sorts of complicated experiments. But if you want to know why a human acts in a certain way all you have to do is ask!

Back to humanism in a moment, but first it should be mentioned that some insist that in biofeedback, holistic health, past-lives therapy, guided fantasy, yoga, transcendental meditation and the like, we have already seen the beginnings of a psychology that may well supersede humanism. So-called fourth-force transpersonalism does mesh with our description of the postmodern world as being one in which Eastern and even tribal religions will be prominent even in Western cultures. For the present, however, humanism is still a dominant force and it is humanism that has impacted the Christian community most significantly.

Christian Counseling: "Now the Problem Is . . . ."

In a way it is not fair to speak of Christian counseling approaches in general terms because of the variety of theories and approaches that are being taken. In another way, it is legitimate to do so because both the popularity and malaise of psychology and counseling have common roots.

In the first place, the discipline experiences criticism because of inadequate integration with biblical theology. In many cases this is not so much because of disinterest in the Bible and theology as because of an inadequate background in theology. It also grows out of the difficulty (some like Jay Adams would say the impossibility!) of integrating secular theories with biblical theology. But perhaps the most decisive factor is that so many Christian counselors and ordinary believers seem to be basically satisfied with a diet of humanism attended by bits and pieces of biblical truth. Reinforced by such biblical notions as "God created us in his own image" and "God doesn't make junk," for example, the Maslowan emphasis on self-esteem, self-actualization and self-fulfillment is tremendously popular and widely used by Christian counselors. A study of eight leading evangelical presses by James Hunter revealed that 87.8 percent of their published titles in 1983 dealt with personal problems and their resolution, self-discovery, self-help and the like (Hunter 1983: 94-98; also see Wells 1992: 174-77). But all of that reckons without the Fall and the kind of "junk" humans have made out of themselves by their rebellion against God—something that has long since been recognized by the likes of David and Isaiah and Paul and Augustine and all who have seen themselves in the light of God's holiness. Self-esteem, like happiness, is a byproduct of something else, not something to be sought in and of itself. For the Christian, at least, it comes by re-creation in Christ and self-denying service, not by climbing upon a pedestal but by taking up a cross.

In our best moments we know all of this. Earlier on Jay E. Adams, Paul C. Vitz and William Kirk Kilpatrick sounded clear warnings. More recently those warnings have been reinforced by Martin and Deidre Bobgan, Richard Ganz, Jim Owen, Larry Crabb, Gary and Carol Almy and others. Psychologist Larry Crabb, for example, takes exception to the self-oriented therapy he himself has employed in the past. In *Finding God* he concludes that increased knowledge of the self rarely leads to richer knowledge of God (Crabb 1993). Psychiatrist Gary Almy and his wife, Carol Tharp Almy, take aim at the "false gospel of psychotherapy" and the recovery movement in their new book *Addicted to Recovery* (Almy and Almy 1994). Like Jay Adams, they believe that it is impossible to reconcile or integrate these approaches with biblical people-helping and they offer biblical correctives. Books such as these lead us to believe that conservative counselors, psychologists and psychiatrists are becoming more and more intent upon developing understandings and approaches that are not only in accord with the Bible but also make better use of it.

In the second place, Christian psychology and counseling as understood and practiced today is profoundly monocultural. It has barely begun the process of integrating Western theory and practice with an understanding of culture and non-Western cultures, even though secular psychology has now made significant strides in dealing with this kind of material. Even apart from theological integration, an understanding of other cultures in and of itself would help to correct excesses brought on by an inordinate emphasis on individualism and the self-orientation of Western culture. Nevertheless, though Christian texts are available, they are not yet widely read and used among conservative psychologists and counselors (cf. Augsburger 1984 and Hesselgrave 1983).

From among counseling approaches that are both biblically and culturally informed, we will focus here on one that illustrates how indispensable Scripture is when dealing with the deepest needs of God's people. It is the approach taken by Timothy Warner, Vice President for International Ministries of Freedom in Christ Ministries of La Habra, California. Accompanied by his wife Eleanor, Warner conducts seminars for churches and missions, and teaches short courses in undergraduate and graduate schools around the world. Warner probably provides counsel and counseling instruction to as many culturally and ethnically diverse people as anyone currently engaged in this type of ministry.

From Tribal Village to Global Village: The Pilgrimage of Timothy Warner

In 1956 Timothy and Eleanor Warner went to West Africa where they served in a tribal village in Sierra Leone under the auspices of the Missionary Church. Both of the Warners had lost their first mates to ill-health and untimely death. After service in Africa they were called to minister at Fort Wayne Bible College. There Timothy Warner served in a variety of capacities. For a while he was chairman of the Department of Missions and then, from 1971 to 1980, president of the college.

After twenty-three years at Fort Wayne, in 1980 the Warners moved to Deerfield, Illinois, where Tim assumed a faculty position in the School of World Mission and Evangelism at Trinity Evangelical Divinity School. After several years he became director of its professional doctoral programs.

From the time of his service in Africa and during his subsequent ministry in North America, Warner became increasingly aware of the fact that Ephesians 6:10-12 is as true today as it was in the day of the apostle Paul. On the surface, the spiritual struggle to which Paul referred takes somewhat different forms in an African village, an Indiana city and a Chicago suburb. But at its core, the struggle is identical, the Enemy is the same, and the resources of God's people do not change.

Throughout the 1980s and into the 1990s Warner became more and more involved with people who had great spiritual and psychological needs—people who were casualties of the warfare between God and Satan, the forces of good and the forces of evil. Together with Eleanor, he ministered to numerous troubled individuals—some of them referred by Christian psychologists and counselors in the Chicago area. In their ministry of people-helping they often resorted to open confrontation with evil spirits and demonic forces, an approach which missiologists refer to as "power encounter." Both as a theorist and practitioner, Warner gained widespread credibility as an authority on spiritual warfare. In 1991, the results of years of study and involvement were set forth in a book on the subject (Warner 1991).

By 1992 the appeals for help from people at home and missionaries and nationals abroad had become so numerous and overwhelming that the Warners were convinced that God was leading them to align themselves with Freedom in Christ Ministries and devote their time and energy to people-helping on an international scale. Having relocated in Ft. Wayne, their schedule now takes them to one city, country and continent after another encouraging, instructing, and delivering God's people as God leads and enables them. In a quite literal sense the world has become their parish.

From Power Encounter
to Truth Encounter

In recent years the primary focus of Warner's thinking

and ministry has gradually shifted from power encounter as such to truth encounter. He is no less convinced that there are times when believers must confront Satan and demonic spirits directly in the name and power of the Lord Jesus, but he has become increasingly aware of the fact that if God's people are to avail themselves of their resources in Christ they must first understand and believe what it means to be *in Christ*.

Warner often quotes one of his college professors who used to say, "People may not live what they profess, but they will always live what they believe." That saying cuts two ways. It means that what people actually do reveals what they really believe. But it also means that what people really believe determines what they actually do. Only Christians who really understand and believe what the Bible says about those who are in Christ have a foundation for coping with the world, for victorious living, and for effective ministry. By definition, then, the truth encounter precedes the power encounter and constitutes preparation for it. The essence of it is expressed in Paul's prayer for the believers in Ephesus (Eph. 1:17-2:7)—a prayer to which Warner refers over and over again.

Truth and Power:
A Manual for Resolving Spiritual Conflicts

In recent years the focus of Warner's ministry has been on helping Christians (and especially Christian pastors and missionaries, and candidates for these ministries) in resolving their own spiritual conflicts as well as in their ministry to others. It is appropriate, therefore, to examine the most salient features of a manual (hereafter referred to as the *Manual*) he has prepared for those who enroll in his seminars and courses entitled *A Manual for Resolving Spiritual Conflicts* (Warner n.d., mimeographed). The *Manual* differs from the book *Spiritual Warfare* in ways that one would expect, but it also reflects the importance of the truth encounter to a greater degree.

In focusing on the *Manual* two cautions are in order. First, the reader should assume that in the nature of the case the *Manual* is subject to continual revision, at least in some of its details. Second, the reader should recognize that no summary as abbreviated as this can do justice to a twenty-eight-page manual chock full of diagrams and biblical references, or to a seminar that deals with a wide variety of illuminating case studies.

Given the fact that the *Manual* has been prepared with Christian workers in view, one might expect that, assuming his students' knowledge of biblical teaching on such subjects as God and Satan, angels and evil spirits, good and evil, and spiritual warfare in the believer and the world, Warner would proceed almost immediately to a consideration of those precise problems most often faced by those who are in ministry. After all, by virtue of careful study and broad experience, Warner is well acquainted with their problems. And pastors and missionaries certainly should know the Bible! The fact that he *does not* assume a good grasp of the basics, even on the part of some of the most gifted, educated and committed members of God's family, goes a long way towards explaining Warner's understanding of the basic reasons for the high incidence of discouragement, depression and defeat among them.

At the same time, Warner does not believe, and Scripture does not teach, that the immediate cause of every case of depression or discouragement or defeat is spiritual defection. But he does believe, and Scripture does teach, that all human ills and difficulties of whatever kind relate to and reflect in some way *the cosmic conflict between God and Satan and therefore the nature of that conflict needs to be clearly understood. It is for that reason that Warner begins where God begins, with biblical teaching about the kind of world we live in, the kind of God we serve, the kind of foe we face, the kind of struggle in which we are engaged, and the kind of resources God has provided.*

To proceed to the *Manual* itself, Warner's approach is

perhaps best understood by reviewing some of the most salient of biblical themes dealt with there and also the sequence or order in which he deals with them.

1) The worldview problem

Consonant with his philosophy that certain central and basic beliefs about the kind of God we serve and the kind of world in which we find ourselves are determinative of the way in which we deal with our problems, Warner begins with worldview. He builds upon Linwood Barney's "layered model" of culture to which we referred earlier (Barney 1973), and also upon Paul Hiebert's theory of the "excluded middle" (Hiebert 1982). The point is that, unlike animists of tribal cultures, Western peoples tend toward a worldview (cosmology or basic belief system—consciously or subconsciously held) that divides the world into two realms, the supernatural (the realm of religion) and the natural (the realm of science). The intermediate spirit world is given little or no consideration at all (it is the "excluded middle," to use Hiebert's term). As a consequence, Westerners ask invalid questions like, "Does it have to do with science *or* religion?" and "Is it a spiritual problem *or* a psychological problem?"

The worldview of animists, on the other hand, projects a single and unified world everywhere and always populated with gods and godlings, good and evil spirits, devils and demons. Successful living is a matter of finding ways and means of appeasing or controlling the spirits.

2) Warfare relationships

Both animistic tribalists and secularized Westerners need the correctives provided by a truly biblical worldview. To be saved, animists especially need to know who Christ is and how he has triumphed over sin and the powers of darkness by his death and resurrection. They need to be set free from the fear of the spirits—a fear that holds them in a vice-like grip.

To be victorious, Western Christians need to take the spirit world much more seriously. They need to be able to recognize the purpose and ploys of Satan and his minions. They need to understand and possess the provision God has made for them in his Son, his Spirit, his ministering angels, and his Word. But more than that, they need to return to biblical teachings concerning God as Creator, Satan as deceiver, Adam and Eve in created and fallen states, the conflict between the dragon and the seed of the woman, the significance of the cross and the resurrection, the nature of Satanic deception, and so on. In the "real world" of the Bible, even Christian believers—and perhaps especially Christian workers—are under attack. Armed with biblical truth and divine authority and power, they need to *go on the attack!*

Warner diagrams the relationship between a biblical worldview and spiritual conflict as in Figure 7 (see Warner n.d.: 8).

3) A daily discipline for renewing the mind

Building on Romans 12:2a, Warner outlines the kind of discipline essential to true discipleship in terms of seven principles.

Principle One: Identify the lies/deceptions from Satan which you have been believing and acting upon.

Principle Two: Reject the lies.

Principle Three: Claim the truth of Scripture for each lie.

Principle Four: Affirm the truth about God and the Lord Jesus Christ.

Principle Five: Review your relationships and release all anger, bitterness, etc., to God.

Principle Six: Put on the whole armor of God.

Principle Seven: Take up the weapon of the Word— "the sword of the Spirit."

Intrinsic to this discipline is a change of focus. As a be-

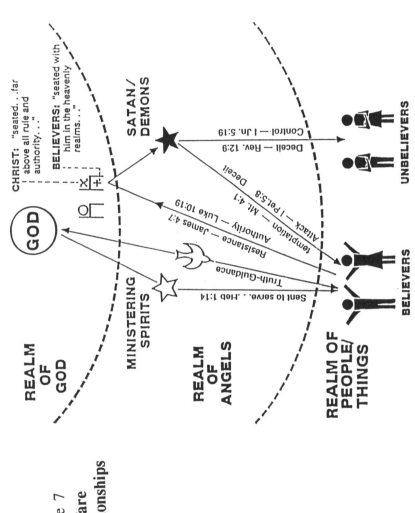

Figure 7
Warfare relationships

liever in Christ, the Christian must direct his/her eyes away from self and on Jesus (Heb. 12:1).

4) The home as a spiritual sanctuary

In courtship, in marriage, in childrearing—in fact, in the whole of family life—it is singularly important in the light of Scripture that the home be a center of instruction, protection, hospitality, ministry and worship. If this is to be the case, both priorities and "procedures" must be very different from those of unbelieving homes because Satan often succeeds in inverting priorities and perverting procedures in human culture. In *Christian* marriage faith and friendship become the foundation for the right physical relationship. In *Christian* homes the husband/father has the primary responsibility for spiritual leadership. Christian homes are to be consecrated and cleansed much as a church is. Warner, therefore, highlights the kind of instruction, prayers, and activities that transform the home into a sanctuary.

5) Steps to freedom in Christ

Finally, in accord with his view that most Christian counseling/people-helping problems result from failure to deal with basic issues in the discipleship process, Warner lays a foundation for counseling in the form of seven steps to freedom in Christ as developed by Neil Anderson, the founder and president of Freedom in Christ Ministries. Every Christian needs to deal with the truth involved in each step—truth from the Bible and truth about one's own life.

Step one: renunciation of false religions.
Step two: deception vs. truth.
Step three: bitterness vs. forgiveness.
Step four: rebellion vs. submission.
Step five: pride vs. humility.
Step six: bondage vs. freedom.
Step seven: acquiescence vs. renunciation.

Conclusion

Some will feel that Warner's background in Africa, his expertise in the animistic worldview, and his prior preoccupation with power encounter all somehow combine to skew his approach to counseling and make him insensitive to the insights of modern psychology. But I would suggest that participation in his seminars and involvement in his therapy sessions on the one hand, and a serious study of the cosmic struggle between God and Satan as revealed in Scripture on the other would serve to temper such criticism. Warner is well acquainted with the relevant literature. He makes numerous references to it in his teaching. He frequently interacts with other specialists, including his own brother who is a prominent psychiatrist.

Again, I would remind the reader that the summary provided here is so succinct as to be of rather limited value in evaluating Warner's approach. But it is sufficient for my present purpose. Namely, to reinforce the kind of biblically-based counseling/people-helping that holds the most hope for church and mission in the future, whether the psychology of the future remains predominantly humanistic or moves in the direction of transpersonalism and the Eastern religions.

Of course, neither Warner nor this writer believes that no problems will remain after Christians have carefully gone through this process, have honestly faced these issues, and have yielded to the guidance of the Holy Spirit. But we do hold that this is where we must begin and that this kind of truth encounter provides a foundation for whatever comes next.

Three simple statements summarize Warner's philosophy in this regard:

1) Counseling is dealing with human beings. The basic resource must therefore be the Scriptures in which God tells us about his creation.

2) A secondary source is the processing of data from the scientific observation of God's creation through what we call general revelation. This source cannot make value judgments, however, so Scripture must always be normative.

3) Most counseling problems in Christians are the result of a failure to deal with basic issues in the discipleship process.

One need only compare Warner's basic approach as we have outlined it with any of a large number of Christian books on problem-solving and people-helping to see the difference that this approach would make in any culture. One aspect of this difference is illustrative and profoundly illuminating, especially as it relates to American culture. *First, recall what we said about the extreme emphasis on self which has been borrowed from humanism and which is foundational to so much of even Christian counseling. Then contrast the approach taken in the* Manual. *There the phrase "I am significant" does not appear until the very last page, and then it is preceded by the phrase "In Christ" (in capital letters), reinforced by a number of Scripture passages, and succeeded by two additional truths—"I am accepted" and "I am secure." The* Manual *begins, not with creation, but with pre-creation. It ends, not with the significance of the self, but with the significance and sufficiency of Christ. And in between, it reconstructs not so much our little stories as the greater story of divine grace and goodness.*

9

John Piper:
Challenging the Church
to World Mission

The traditional word was "exhort." In New Testament Greek it is *parakaleo*—to "call near," i.e., to invite, invoke, entreat, beseech. But the contemporary word seems to be "challenge."

It has been said that church leaders have done a much better job of *challenging* Christians to good works and Christian witness than they have in *channeling* them in work and witness. Generally speaking, that is probably true. But it may not be true when it comes to Christian missions. In evangelical circles at least, not only has the call to mission been loud and clear; opportunities for missionary involvement have been many and varied. Nevertheless, as we have come to know it, the missionary challenge cries out for reexamination.

Contemporary calls to missionary commitment usually are directed to one or more of three types of motivation: obedience to the commands of Scripture (principally but not solely the Great Commission), meeting the desperate needs of people (primarily spiritual but including all kinds of needs), and involvement in an exciting and winning cause (being "where the action is," participating in a cause that will ultimately triumph). Down through the years challenges of these types have been relatively effective in motivating Western churches to support Christian missions around the world. In more recent years, and largely motivated by the same kinds of appeals, many of the younger churches of the Third World themselves have initiated significant missionary endeavors.

If, then, the call to mission has been effective both West and East, and North and South, why subject it to scrutiny at this late date in the history of church and mission?

The answer is really quite simple. *Underlying these challenges is something still more basic—something that lends meaning and urgency to all such appeals. Namely, the perception, purpose and plan of Almighty God. Divorced, or even temporarily separated, from HIS all-encompassing understandings and undertakings, appeals such as these lose their ultimate significance and may actually become counterproductive.*

Some years ago now one seminarian expressed his concern about typical missionary challenges in the following manner (as closely as I can recall):

> Sometimes I grow weary of going to missionary conferences, drinking missionary firewater, and returning home to regurgitate, only to be invited to return for more firewater. Unless the Spirit speaks I sometimes fear that missionary activists will only succeed in turning me off on missions. The Spirit speaks through Scripture I am told.

His reaction may have been extreme, but nevertheless it is worth pondering.

Human Invention or Divine Intention?

Perhaps the age-old question "Does the end justify the means?" pertains here. We may not see its relevance because the inherent goodness and greatness of the church's missionary task sometimes obscure the problem. When this happens, biblical principles yield to blatant pragmatism, divine intention to human invention. In the vast majority of cases, it is not the conscious intent of missionary recruiters and promoters to mislead the Christian public. It is just that the needs are so many, the opportunities are so great, and the time is so short that even though there may be an occasional twinge of conscience over lack of depth and objectivity in our preaching and reporting, it is quickly quieted by the assurance that God's hand is in this entire enterprise and therefore all appeals are justified.

There comes to my mind a cartoon I saw a number of years ago now. It pictured a missionary speaker about to take his turn on the podium. As he left the pew he turned to a missionary colleague and queried, "Shall we tell them the truth or keep them happy?" That captures something of the dilemma, though the alternatives are not quite that stark and simple. Nevertheless, it must be admitted that missionary challenges do not always take the high road.

Consider briefly some of the ways in which human invention can obscure divine intention in communicating missionary challenges of the three types mentioned above.

1) Obedience to the Great Commission

On the face of it, simple obedience to what our Lord has commanded may seem to be the most uncomplicated and purest form of motivation for participation in the world mission of the church. Even in this case, however, the command can be misrepresented or misinterpreted so as to make it subservient to our special interests and undertakings. For example, in spite of textual and exegetical problems, the Marcan statement of the Commission (Mark 16:15-20) has been used to support the notion that attesting miracles *must* accompany the preaching of the gospel. In spite of the emphasis on authoritative sending in the text, the Johannine statement (John 20:21) has been used to support the idea that political and social action is an equal partner with evangelism in the Great Commission. And in spite of a grammatical construction that binds the whole world together as the immediate arena of mission, Acts 1:8 has been used to challenge churches to concentrate on their "Jerusalem" before considering overseas missions.

2) Meeting the needs of humankind

I recall the stirring address of a prominent evangelical professor upon his return from Africa several years ago. He related how Africans had crowded around the airplane as he was about to take off. One mother especially was pressing toward the window and pointing to her sickly child. With great passion he explained how, after taking off, he said to the pilot, "I've just seen Jesus. I've just seen Jesus." Then, referring to Jesus' words to the effect that when we care for these little ones we care for Jesus himself (Matt. 25:40), he made an impassioned appeal for funds for medical work in that African country. Of course, the cause itself was legitimate and the use of Matthew 25 for this kind of appeal is a common one. But careful exegesis simply will not sustain it.

This brings to mind the results of some recent research by James F. Engel and his associates. According to this research, whereas their forebears had an abiding concern for evangelism and church-planting in the "regions beyond," baby-boomers tend to favor a "holistic" mission that is more socially oriented and starts "right here at home." This indicates that there will be an increasing problem when it comes to raising support for missions among baby-boomers. Engel's solution is to make a corresponding adjustment in the way we view and promote missions in the future (Engel 1990). From a pragmatic perspective, that solution seems incontrovertible. However, lest we mistake God's priorities, perhaps both baby-boomers and their elders together should take a more careful look at the biblical text!

3) Involvement in an exciting and winning cause

Make no mistake about it. From a Christian perspective no cause is greater than that of proclaiming the gospel to our world and inviting its peoples to become citizens of the Kingdom. Nor does any cause have an outcome that is more hopeful and certain. Unfortunately those truths are easily transmuted into appeals that are suspect. The missionary volunteer who responded to a short-term opportunity in Eastern Europe by exclaiming "I think I'll go. It sounds like fun" was misled in the same way as the recruit who signs on with the Navy after viewing the sign "Join the Navy and see the world."

So are all those who are overly impressed by statistics which point to the great growth of the church worldwide. Growth there is, but statistics can conceal as much as they reveal. Over a decade ago some church growth analysts projected general population and church growth rates of sub-Saharan Africa into the future and confidently predicted that Africa would be a Christian continent by the year 2000. For a while all eyes were trained on Africa. Optimism and enthusiasm were everywhere evident. Africa as a mission field was elevated on the agenda of churches and missions. Now we know more about the problems of both the nations and the churches of Africa. Intertribal strife is everywhere evident. And even many evangelical churches are plagued by lingering ties to questionable tribal customs and witchcraft. As a result, churches and missions in Africa receive much less attention though the challenge is greater than ever! Bandwagons are not recommended conveyances if one really wants to go somewhere.

Now a word of caution. By no means are the above lines to be interpreted as questioning the necessity of obedience to Christ and responding to human need, or as an indictment of short-term missions and statistical analysis. Not at all. But there is a better way to challenge the church. There is a missionary motivation that holds more potential and promise. There is an understanding of both church and mission that runs deeper. To that we now turn.

John Piper:
The Supremacy and Glory of God in Mission

Not a few church and mission leaders have grounded the missionary calling and motivation in the nature of God and the church as revealed in Scripture. Writings of Johannes Verkuyl, J. Robertson McQuilkin, Arthur Glasser, Herbert J. Kane, Don Richardson and Steven Hawthorne, among others, readily come to mind. That is all to the good. But it must be admitted that when it comes to the world mission of the church, all too often pastors and leaders of our congregations leave the task of instructing and challenging God's people to others. That in itself is quite discouraging. But the problem is compounded when missions people who inherit that opportunity by default are not given the time, or do not have the ability or inclination, to go about it in the best way.

Happily, there are many exceptions to this state of affairs. One such is Minneapolis's Bethlehem Baptist Church where John Piper is senior pastor. I stress "pastor" because that fact in itself is important to my present purpose.

Piper is no ordinary pastor and Bethlehem Baptist is not your average church. Piper has a doctorate in theology from the University of Munich. He and his family (in fact, most of the church staff) live within walking distance of their inner-city church. Piper has been actively involved in writing, in lecturing and preaching elsewhere, and in anti-abortion and other social causes in Minneapolis, in addition to ministering to the local congregation. And at the heart of all that he does in writing, preaching and ministering is a concern for the supremacy of God in church and mission. Perhaps a part of the secret to understanding both Piper's mind and heart is to be found in his words:

> I have to admit that most of my soul's food comes from very old books. I find the atmosphere of my own century far too dense with man and distant from the sweet sovereignty of God (Piper 1991: 14).

Little wonder that, according to *World Pulse* (Vol. 28, No.5; Feb. 12, 1993), Bethlehem Baptist is ranked seventh in the list of the top twenty missions churches in the United States; has an organized group of some fifty or sixty people who meet regularly with an eye to missionary service; devotes one-third of its budget to support the missionary program; is a center for those who want to enroll in the World Christian Movement course inaugurated by the U.S. Center for World Mission. That is not to say that the church has had no problems, nor that it will have no problems in the future. On the contrary, one might expect that Satan will take aim on a church with this kind of vision and outreach. At the same time, the success of the church and its pastoral staff has been outstanding even in the kind of geographical location being vacated by many churches.

Let the Nations be Glad!

As a theologian-pastor, John Piper has written on a variety of topics—the art of preaching, the doctrine of justification, the basics of Christian living, the teaching of the Synoptics and more. But for our purposes perhaps the most revealing work is a recent one entitled *Let the Nations be*

Glad!: The Supremacy of God in Missions (1993). In the preface of that book, Piper opens his heart and mind to the scrutiny of his readers. What he writes cannot be expressed in a more poignant way than he has already expressed it:

> This book is a partial payment of a debt I owe to the nations. . . . To those culturally near me and those culturally far I am a debtor. Not because they gave me anything that I must pay back, but because God gave me what can't be paid back. He gave me the all-satisfying pleasure of knowing him and being loved by him through his Son Jesus Christ.
>
> . . . .
>
> I have said to the missionaries of our church, "Your devotion has a tremendous power in my life. Your leaving is a means of my staying. Your strengths make up for my weaknesses. Your absence empowers my presence. So I thank God for you. May God make the reciprocity of our motivation more and more effective in the years to come." But the [this] book is not just for missionaries. It's for pastors who (like me) want to connect their fragile, momentary, local labors to God's invincible, eternal, global purposes. It's for lay people who want a bigger motivation for being world Christians than they get from statistics. It's for college and seminary classes on the theology of missions that really want to be theological as well as anthropological, methodological and technological. And it's for leaders who need the flickering wick of their vocation fanned into flame again with a focus on *the Supremacy of God in missions* (Piper 1993: 8-9; emphasis his).

What a word that is. And how humbling to even those of us who have devoted years to the mission field and the mission classroom!

But it is not so much the testimony in the preface but the substance of the book itself that is crucial to our thesis here. *Namely, that it is the Word of God itself that provides the basic context, content, and correctives that the Spirit uses to guide and guard us in global mission.* These are not, of course, mutually exclusive categories. They intertwine considerably so that, at times, any one of them becomes inextricable from the others. But they do furnish us with one way of getting at what Piper says and does in this book so I will employ them here.

First, then, to the *context.*

The Bible is the context of mission. I know that that sounds strange. And it is not Piper's phrase. It is mine. To be sure, the context of mission is the world, but it is the world as that world is seen by God—the world first of all in joyful subjection to its Creator, then in rebellion and conflict, and, ultimately, the world restored to a glad relationship with its Sovereign God. It is not the world as worldlings view the world that is really the context of mission. It is not even the world as we Christians might be tempted to view the world. It is the world as God views the world that is missions' real context—the world defined and described in the Bible, the biblical world of which our contemporary world is an extension.

The primary question in missions, then, is not "What in the *world* is God doing?" but "What in the *Word* is God doing?" What he is doing in the world is what we find him doing first in the Word. Piper understands that, though he does not express it in this way. Why do I say it that way? Because, by my calculations there are well over 600 Scripture references in this book of but 228 pages. Of course, even that can be misleading. Gustavo Gutierezz has about 425 Bible references in his book *Liberation Theology* but the picture he paints of the world, and its problem and its solution, is still very different from that which is revealed in the Bible. So it is important to add that Piper does not just *refer* to Scripture. He *responds* to Scripture. He does not *wrest from* the text; he *rests in* the text.

That makes for both a world of difference and a different world because, as we have said, the biblical world is a world that begins and ends with God—with both the supremacy of God and the worship of him. So, though we have not always looked at things that way, Piper is essentially correct when he writes:

> Missions is not the ultimate goal of the church. Worship is. Missions exists [*sic*] because worship doesn't. Worship is ultimate, not missions, because God is ultimate, not man. When this age is over, and the countless millions of the redeemed fall on their faces before the throne of God, missions will be no more. It is a temporary necessity. But worship abides forever. Worship, therefore, is the fuel and goal in missions. It's the goal of missions because in missions we simply aim to bring the nations into the white-hot enjoyment of God's glory. The goal of missions is the gladness of the peoples in the greatness of God. "The Lord reigns; let the earth *rejoice*; let the many coastlands *be glad* (Psalm 97:1). "Let the peoples praise thee, O God; let all the peoples praise thee! Let the nations *be glad and sing for joy!* (Psalm 67:3-4) (Piper 1993, 11; emphasis his).

So if we begin with a beneficent but benign God looking down at a wayward world and compassionately considering what he might do to rescue his creatures and creation, we've got the wrong starting-point for understanding mission. Mission begins with the supremacy and glory of a "God in relentless pursuit of praise and honor from creation to consummation" (Piper 1993: 17). The God of the Bible looks on his world as a jealous God who will not share his glory with another. Jealous, not as though he needs us. Jealous because only when God is God to all his creatures can the world be put on its true Axis.

Next we come to *content*.

Without even the thought of doing justice to the content of a book absolutely crammed with the really solid stuff of missions, I would simply point again to the central theme of the supremacy of God in the Word and world and provide two intimations of how the text of the Bible informs the content of Piper's book.

The content of *Let the Nations Be Glad* is first of all extensive. The grand sweep of the biblical perspective on mission is both prescribed and preserved. The blurb on the back cover says that Piper deals with key biblical texts. He does that. But he does more than deal with important but unconnected texts. He literally marches through four solid pages of biblical texts to show how, at all times and in every situation, God has demonstrated zeal for his own glory (Piper 1993: 17-21). When Piper sets out to show how the early church called upon God in prayer to the end that God be glorified in his world, he devotes almost five solid pages to make his case (Piper 1993: 56-61). Of course, no author can simply pile up verse upon verse (not just the reference, but also the text). Nevertheless, the Bible itself supplies a great part of the content of this book quantitatively.

The content is also intensive. Over and over, Piper faces really tough and contemporary missiological questions such as those having to do with the meaning of *ethne*, the definition of "unreached peoples," the complementarity of the various statements of the Great Commission, and the necessity of repenting and believing in Christ. These and similar issues are met head-on and analyzed biblically. And this not by a missiologist as such but by a pastor-theologian. And not for the seminary classroom alone but for all God's people who are or should be concerned for God's work in the world.

So here we have both breadth and depth of content. Could it be that too many of us underestimate the capacity of too many of God's people too much of the time? It would seem so from a reading of this book.

Finally, we come to *correctives.*

David Wells charges that evangelicals have lost the power of dissent (1992: 288). Not Piper. He refuses to capitulate to clichés like "Missions work is the greatest activity in the world" and "Prayer is THE work of missions." He does not run away from themes like suffering and judgment. He takes issue with the proposals of prominent people—the universalism of George MacDonald and the pluralism of John Hick. He even takes issue with the conclusions of some fellow evangelicals. Piper is thorough-going in his criticism of Clark Pinnock, John Stott and Edward Fudge for defining hell, not as a place of eternal punishment, but as an "event of annihilation." And he takes issue with Millard Erickson and Norman Anderson who have espoused the idea that people can be saved apart from conscious knowledge and belief in Jesus Christ.

By the way, it is important to note that Piper does not oppose these scholars on the basis that such teachings cut the umbilical cord of missions and rob the church of missionary motivation. No, he opposes them on the basis that their views do not square with the biblical text. And he does so courteously and Christianly as well as (many will be persuaded) conclusively. In the process Piper rescues significant motivations for mission. But he does so almost as a byproduct of loyalty to the text itself.

Conclusion

If it were true that Piper is falling on his face as pastor, that he were not in demand as a preacher and teacher, and that his writings had little market and impact, then I might at least waver in my confidence—not in the potential of the Word to convict and challenge God's people, but in the capacity of contemporary congregations to hear and respond to it. But Piper's record, and my own confidence and experience, lead in another direction. I am fully persuaded that the farther our runaway world gets from the Bible the closer the church and mission must get to it—not just for information, but for sustenance and strength.

I recall speaking in a Florida church on one occasion when my professor in the lone missions course offered during my seminary days was present. She had been an outstanding missionary in China before the Communist takeover. I had just been to Hong Kong and, impressed with what was being done among refugees and orphans, I recounted some of my experiences. After the service she kindly commended and then cautioned me. I had forgotten most of what she said in the classroom before my pastoral and missionary career began. But I have never forgotten what she said on that occasion in Florida. She said:

> David, you must have noticed how moved the congregation was when you spoke about the orphanage and the work among refugees from China. But did you also notice that the handkerchiefs went back into the pockets and pocketbooks when you spoke about evangelism and the churches? It's alright to speak about physical and social needs. But the most important thing is that people get a vision for preaching the gospel and building the church among Chinese. Try to find ways to get God's people more concerned about the spiritual condition of Hong Kong's people than anything else.

I have learned that there is no better way to do this— perhaps no other way—than placing mission squarely in the context of Scripture. Piper points us in that direction. Unlike Don Richardson, Steven Hawthorne and others, he does not re-tell the "Bible story" as such. (At least, he does not do so in this book.) But in another way he does "tell the story" because all of the ingredients are here—the cast of characters, the plot, the development, and the resolution. It's just that they are connected differently, sometimes chronologically but always thematically. So, aside from narrative form, it is all here.

And if and when other visions move us in the wrong direction or to less worthy pursuits—or if they fail to move us at all—we could do no better than join Piper in a reconsideration of the biblical text and see again that which supersedes all of "our" worlds—ancient, modern, postmodern. Because

> God is pressing us further into the humblest and deepest experience of his grace, and weaning us more and more from our ingrained pride. In doing this he is preparing for himself a people—from all the peoples—who will be able to worship him with free and white-hot admiration.
>
> Therefore the church is bound to engage with the Lord of Glory in his cause. It is our unspeakable privilege to be caught up with him in the greatest movement in history—the ingathering of the elect "from all tribes and tongues and peoples and nations" until the full number of Gentiles come in, and all Israel is saved, and the Son of Man descends with power and great glory as King of kings and Lord of lords and the earth is full of the knowledge of his glory as the waters cover the sea for ever and ever. Then the supremacy of Christ will be manifest to all and he will deliver the kingdom to God the Father and God will be all in all (Piper 1993: 223).

Let us agree, then, that witness is at the center of the reason for our being here. *But worship is at the center of the reason for our being anywhere!*

10

Ralph D. Winter:
Consecrating and Training
Future Leaders

In several places the New Testament speaks of *gifts to persons*: i.e., spiritual gifts that are given to believers (cf. Rom. 12; 1 Cor. 12-14). In one place it also refers to *"person gifts"*: i.e., apostles, prophets, evangelists and pastor-teachers given by the ascended Christ to his church (Eph. 4:11). These "person gifts" have a primary responsibility for "building the church" and "building *up* " the church—equipping believers for service, bringing them to oneness in faith, increasing their knowledge of Christ, maturing them in Christian living, and keeping them from being "blown away" by human trickery and teaching (Eph. 4:12-16).

As Lord of the church, Christ knew that it needed leaders. Though these leaders are referred to as "gifts" only in this one place, Christ provides them on a continuing basis in order that the church might continue to "go and grow." Accordingly, after writing about the qualifications of church leaders in his first letter, in his second letter to Timothy Paul instructed him very specifically to pass on what he had learned to faithful men who would be able to teach still others (2 Tim. 2:2). There is indeed an "apostolic succession" in the New Testament. But it consists not so much in an unbroken succession of "prelates" who direct the "affairs" of the church as it does in an unbroken line of "person gifts" who pass on the "faith" of the church. Therefore, apart from Anglo-Catholics and a few others, Protestants in general do not give a whole lot of attention to apostolic succession as such, but they do give considerable attention to keeping the faith and training the faithful. Institutions of various sizes and types, organizations within and without the church, programs and strategies of greater or lesser significance, manuals and books large and small—all are dedicated to Sunday School and Bible study curricula, discipleship and teacher preparation, professional and lay training, and theological and Christian liberal arts education.

Obviously it would be a herculean task to analyze and evaluate an educational/training enterprise as vast and complex as this. But two preliminary observations are incontrovertible. First, the church and its missions now provide unprecedented learning opportunities for their members (and outsiders as well). Second, progress has come at a high price. Our approach here, then, will be to highlight a few basic problems that have been isolated by astute observers and then underscore some correctives which have been suggested recently.

Identifying and Consecrating Spiritual Leaders

We begin by building upon a biblical distinction already apparent from a reading of previous chapters and the paragraphs above. The distinction is this: as disciples, learners, saints, and people of God, *all* believers are to be trained to serve; as leaders, teachers, trainers and person gifts of Christ, *some* believers are to be set apart and prepared for leadership roles.

In contemporary Christian thinking "discipleship" is quite ambiguous but usually refers to selecting certain believers and training them in ways to live out their faith and win others. But it is more biblical to think of discipleship quite differently. As we have seen, the grammatical construction of the Great Commission in Matthew 28:16-20 indicates that we are to "disciple" the nations by going with the gospel, baptizing those who turn to Christ, and teaching *all* who are baptized *all* that Christ has commanded. *All* believers are to be discipled. *Some* believers are to be set apart for specialized roles in missionizing, evangelizing, preaching, pastoring and teaching. *All* believers are to be built up in the faith and equipped to serve. *Some* disciples will be set apart for service as "equippers."

So the question is, how are these "specialist-equippers" to be identified and set aside for special training and service? Consider the difference between New Testament and contemporary practices in this regard. In an illuminating piece written some years ago, Michael Griffith pointed out that there is no general appeal for missionary volunteers in the New Testament, for example. Every missionary in the New Testament was either called directly by Christ or personally appointed by Holy Spirit-led leaders and churches (Griffith 1967: 20-21). The same seems to have been true of New Testament leadership in general. Leaders and laity alike waited upon the Lord, took account of the quality of one another's life and gifts, and then consecrated leaders who had already qualified on the basis of faith, faithfulness and fruitfulness.

In contemporary Christian practice it is quite different. We tend to challenge all Christians, not just to serve Christ, but to volunteer as candidates for specialized ministries in church and mission, go to this or that school in order to prepare themselves, and then *present themselves* for ministry. Having done all of that, churches and missions are more or less obligated to employ and deploy these volunteers unless or until they prove themselves unworthy. Of course there are exceptions, but while the biblical norm was to encourage *all* believers to deny self, take up their cross, and commit themselves completely to Christ and his cause, only in certain cases did this eventuate in being selected and consecrated for special ministries in church and mission. Leaders were singled out from among the larger "company of the committed" by people other than themselves.

Theological Education in North America

Those who have spent a large part of their lives in schools—first as students, then as teachers or administrators—are sometimes called upon to reflect on the progress of American education and evaluate present programs. If one begins at the beginning, it becomes an enlightening enterprise.

Harvard is one of the most prestigious universities in the world today, but it began in the seventeenth century with one teacher/president and one student. Early students were barely in their teens with little previous schooling. The main study was Latin because to know Latin was to be literate. Those who were going into the ministry learned Latin at Harvard and then were trained as apprentices in the pastorate (see Winter 1994: 39).

In the past three centuries both education in general and theological education in particular have become more and more extensive and specialized. For good or ill—or good *and* ill—even our top seminaries face unprecedented challenges.

First, more often than not the student body today is a mixed group. Some students are in seminary to "find themselves" and their place in the world. Some are professionals in secular fields who want biblical and theological training or who are considering a vocational change. Some seek specialized training for church-related professions. Some already feel called to the pastorate, evangelism or missions. Some entering students have very little background in church life itself. Only a few bring with them a significant knowledge of the Scriptures. An increasing number of students come from the Third

World (especially Asia) and bring with them very different backgrounds and limited facility in the English language. In the nature of the case, the burden upon an educational institution to meet the needs of a student body of such diversity is a heavy one indeed.

Second, given the size of the average student body and these complexities, it has become increasingly difficult to foster and monitor the spiritual growth of students. Several years ago, a prominent Chinese professor publicly berated our American seminaries for providing the kind of education that bestowed honors upon graduates on the basis of their grade point average alone. His point was that on that basis the seminary undoubtedly was guilty of honoring some students whose spirituality was at a lower level at the time they left school than it was when they first entered it!

Third, with the explosion of knowledge and the increase in specialized training programs, seminary curricula and instruction tend to become fragmented and unintegrated. David Wells, himself a seminary professor, puts it this way:

> Subjects and fields develop their own literatures, working assumptions, vocabularies, technical terms, criteria for what is true and false, and canons of what literature and what views should be common knowledge among those working in the subjects. The result of this is a profound increase in knowledge but often an equally profound loss in understanding what it all means, how it is all interconnected, how knowledge in one field should inform that in another. This is the bane of every seminarian's existence. The dissociated fields—biblical studies, theology, church history, homiletics, ethics, pastoral psychology, missiology— become a rain of hard pellets relentlessly bombarding those who are on the pilgrimage to graduation. Students are left more or less defenseless as they run this gauntlet, supplied with little help in their efforts to de-

termine how to relate the fields one to another. In the end, the only warrant for their having to endure the onslaught is that somehow and someday it will all come together in a church (Wells 1992: 244-45).

Fourth, in many seminaries there is a strong tendency for the social sciences to overshadow biblical and theological studies. The Bible we have with us always; the sciences always come up with something new. And, like ancient Athenian society, our society is enamored with anything that is "new." It is with a great deal of validity that Edward Rommen writes about the "detheologization of missiology" (Rommen 1993). Returning to David Wells, he writes concerning *Leadership* magazine, a publication designed to aid evangelical pastors. He indicates that less than one percent of all essays appearing in *Leadership* between 1980 and 1988 contained any reference to the Bible even though the Bible treats many of the topics dealt with in the various articles (Wells 1992: 177).

Fifth, the cost of building adequate facilities, procuring library resources, hiring qualified faculties and otherwise providing for educational programs of this magnitude is rapidly becoming prohibitive. A significant part of these costs become the responsibility of the students themselves. As a result, pressures on students and their spouses increase, graduation day is postponed and student loans skyrocket. It is not unusual for students to graduate with accumulated debts of fifteen to twenty thousand dollars or more. Such a debt has serious and negative consequences upon ministry options and, indeed, upon ministry itself.

While there is no panacea for these and still other problems in our seminaries (and undergraduate schools as well), certain innovations have been designed with a view to preserving advances, ameliorating problems and forging ahead in theological education. Supervised internships, enhanced student-adviser relationships, team-taught courses, scholarships, in-service educational opportunities and much more represent attempts to deal with problems such as those we have identified here.

Training Christian Leaders
in the Third World

In the middle of the nineteenth century after but one generation of missions from North America, the Congregational missiologist Rufus Anderson visited Asia. One thing that impressed him was the growth of educational and other institutions. Another was the scarcity of qualified national pastors.

A little over a century later, some Presbyterian missionaries in Central America surveyed their own situation and that of the younger churches in general. What they saw certainly represented significant gains over the century that separated them from Rufus Anderson. But there were still some ominous gaps that obviously had to be "filled in" if church and mission were to move forward.

First, there was the gap between the training of the average pastor and the needs of the churches and their fledgling missions. Most pastors, especially those in denominations and fellowships where churches were multiplying most rapidly, had very little formal theological training, if any. In fact, many were simply laymen who were called upon to serve as pastors in addition to carrying on other lines of work.

Second, there was the gap between the residential schools and the church leadership. On the one hand, those who had already proved to be gifted and faithful in ministry could not uproot themselves and their families, locate in the area of the Bible school or seminary for an extended period of time, and continue to support the family while carrying on their studies. On the other hand, younger unmarried volunteers for training and service often completed their education only to go into more lucrative occupations. Even when they went into the ministry, they sometimes proved to be unsuitable because of inexperience and an education that was divorced from village life.

Third, there tended to be a persistent gap between the curricula of the training schools and the concerns of the indigenous culture. Missionary teachers—and, often, national instructors as well—were trained in Europe or North America. Courses of study, textbooks and reference books, and even class notes, study outlines and examinations—all were imported with the teachers. Missionary instructors could not be expected to deal with aspects of the local culture that they did not really understand. National instructors often did not deal with local beliefs and customs which they associated with their pre-Christian past and, in any case, had not been germane to their advanced and foreign education.

Now it should be made clear that problems such as these were not unique to Central America. They were world problems. And they were addressed by educators across the ecclesiastical spectrum. In the conciliar movement, those who managed the Theological Education Fund for the World Council of Churches developed three major programs designed to upgrade libraries in Third World theological schools, provide advanced educational opportunities for their faculties, and encourage the formation of contextualized theologies. We have already noted the mixed results of these efforts in the chapter on contextualization.

For their part, conservatives cooperated in the development of advanced training institutions in key centers such as Nairobi, Bangui, Manila and Tokyo. In addition, through the efforts of leaders such as Paul Bowers in Africa, Bong Rin Ro in Asia, and others, regional accrediting associations were formed in order to elevate standards of theological education. Heading up the educational arm of The World Evangelical Fellowship, William Taylor is making significant contributions to the advancement of theological education throughout the Third World. Under the leadership of Robert Coleman, the Institute of Evangelism at the Billy Graham Center has prepared and distributes self-study courses for Christian leaders around the world. The goal is to help leaders evangelize the lost, establish new Christians and equip growing Christians for ministry. And this is only the beginning!

Theological Education: the Innovations of Ralph D. Winter

If those who are familiar with educational developments in the non-Western Christian world were asked to look back over the years since World War II and designate the one innovation that has been most significant, in all likelihood they would answer, "Theological Education by Extension" (TEE). If the same people were then asked to nominate the one person who has been most influential in terms of enhancing theological education and making it more widely available to leaders and potential leaders of church and mission, in all likelihood many would respond, "Ralph Winter."

Winter was one of a coterie of educational leaders in Central America who, in the postwar years, took a long, hard look at pastoral selection and training on the one hand, and the needs of the churches on the other. Jim Emery was another. Actually, Emery was there first and contributed the key insight: the real leaders were in the congregations, not in the seminary student bodies! Winter then helped to figure out how these leaders could be trained, focusing first on training church leaders for Guatemalan Indians.

These field missionaries concluded that those in the Pentecostal tradition had in fact rediscovered an important strategy in allowing ministry opportunity to gifted leaders without extensive special training. While not wanting to give up their tradition of formal training, their goal was to make training available to the real leaders in the local congregations. *Thus, TEE was born with more of an emphasis on whom to teach than on what to teach.*

Winter became Executive Director of ALET, the Latin American Association of Theological Schools (Northern Region), and in that capacity spread the "TEE gospel" in the seventeen northernmost countries of Latin America. In 1965 he was invited south where he encouraged TEE thinking and was in attendance at the birth of a Brazilian association of seminaries in extension. Subsequently, under the auspices of the EFMA and in the company of Ralph Covell, he embarked upon a global trip during which no less than eighty-three seminaries were visited and introduced to TEE. Since that time many schools have inaugurated TEE programs. At the same time, many of them oppose the ordination of those leaders who complete them. Winter feels that this is a betrayal of the original insights and purpose of TEE.

During the last twenty-five to thirty years, Winter has been active and innovative in other ways. He saw the need for a publishing ministry that would give priority to mission materials and established William Carey Library. He saw the need for the kind of training that would better prepare students who were in the throes of considering missions as a major career, and initiated the Perspectives Study Course. He believed there was a need for a major mission center in each country, and inaugurated the U.S. Center for World Mission which became a model for some thirty such centers around the world. He felt there was a need for an experimental university in association with the U.S. Center and originated William Carey University.

In all of this, Winter has not lost sight of the fundamental leadership crisis that has arisen as evangelical churches and educational institutions place an increased emphasis on the professional ministry. He has pointed out that, except in Pentecostal movements around the world, the usual mission field has a hundred churches and only ten "properly trained pastors." Consequently, he and his associates have developed the World Christian Foundations (WCF) curriculum aimed at upgrading the training of leaders already in place and functioning as pastors in the ninety congregations rather than working toward re-placing them with "young men trained in school rather than real life." In order to avoid what would have been significant resistance to curriculum change, TEE concentrated on delivery systems—getting training to those who most needed it. Now when many schools are initiating new programs and changes in their curricula, WCF aims to take the most beneficial kind of education to those who are in a position to make good use of it.

Beyond TEE: The World Christian Foundations Course of Study

As we entered the 1990s, Winter began to think more and more about two gigantic obstacles to the completion of the Great Commission in the foreseeable future, and also about a tremendous pool of potential workers who could spearhead an unprecedented breakthrough. The way he viewed it, the "two largest obstacles to missions from the U.S.A." are rather easily identifiable:

> what is the largest obstacle. . . ? It is very simply the tragic, trudging, procession of college graduates who are too burdened with debts to allow them to go into missions. School debts interpose years of delay—and usually end in denial—of the mission call for tens of thousands of mission-minded college graduates!
>
> The second-largest obstacle . . . is the fact that our society has unthinkingly chosen to impose what seems to be endless years of schooling before young people can enter into real life, jobs, marriage, etc. This means missionaries arrive on the field ten years older and far less able to master the language. Or, in 90% of the cases, these thousands of once-enthusiastic mission-minded students don't arrive at all (Winter 1994: 3).

But Winter seldom sees problems without coming up with solutions as well. The solution to overcoming these two obstacles is to be found in tapping into a huge pool of potential missionaries. First, by 1993 the Perspectives course had been completed by some 20,000 Christians in the United States and an equal number in other countries. Some 80,000 others had been exposed to *Perspectives on the World Christian Movement* (Winter and Hawthorne 1981), the textbook used in that course. The vast majority of these people have had their appetites whetted for further study and Christian service. Winter sees them as a vast pool of possible Christian workers.

Second, it has not escaped his notice that there are an estimated forty million Americans over the age of twenty-five who have only two years of college and that five million of them are now enrolled in off-campus degree completion programs. According to Winter's calculations, this means that there are over 200,000 evangelicals who could be candidates for full- and part-time Christian service if a WCF-type curriculum were made available to them in a "degree completion mode" by Christian colleges across the country.

So Winter's solution is twofold. Missions should give serious consideration to accepting candidates from among these hundreds of thousands who have been considered "unavailable" because they have not yet completed college. And churches, missions and individual Christians should give a larger place to Bible-based, off-campus education.

To expedite this solution, Winter and his able associates—his wife Roberta, William Osborne, James Oliver Buswell III, and Corinne Armstrong among others—have developed a thirty-two-semester-unit curriculum called World Christian Foundations. Currently available on an experimental basis directly from the Institute for International Studies of the U.S. Center, it is primarily being prepared for use by other schools around the world in their off-campus programs. Already a number of Third World schools are adopting it, as are several major U.S. seminaries. The new field surveyors division of Wycliffe Bible Translators is suggesting that a graduate-level version also be made available in the near future.

The reader may be forgiven for responding, "Just what I thought! Another study course, and a long one at that!" But there is more here than meets the eye. A lot more. So if the reader is interested in Christian education that is truly Christian, and in resolving many of the problems and overcoming the obstacles referred to above (that should include about all of us), he or she should be sure to read on—carefully and prayerfully! As in previous chapters, we cannot go into great detail. But there is no need to do so in the present context. Complete information is available from the Institute for International Studies. Anyway, our basic purpose is not to promote any one course of study as such, but rather to point to innovations which may be adopted and adapted to other studies and situations—innovations which hold special promise for church and mission in a postmodern age.

The primary features of the World Christian Foundations course of study, then, are as follows:

1) *A Field-based Design.* Whereas on-campus programs of the kind that characterize traditional Bible college and seminary programs require that students (and often spouses and children) relocate in the area of the school, WCF allows them to remain in the area of employment and church involvement. Whereas off-campus programs such as those sponsored in TEE and many other extension courses often require professors to meet with students at a distance from the main campus, WCF requires personal input from only one mentor and allows for more flexibility as to meeting places and times of meeting.

2) *A Missionary Perspective.* More often than not, Christian education, including training in Bible and theology, focus on either the subject matter of the particular course of study and/or the particular type of ministry envisioned by the student. The student who is preparing for a pastoral ministry, for example, takes systematic theology and pastoral theology.

In systematics the student examines what the Bible says about the nature of God, the fall of man, the means of grace, the church, and so on. In pastoral theology the student focuses on preaching, administration, officiating at weddings and funerals, etc. What is all too easily lost in all of this is the overall purpose and plan of God, and the progress of his plan through the ages. Also overlooked, or at least minimized, are such things as the global church, world religions, the impact of culture, and so on. The very theme of the WCF curriculum, on the other hand, is "Declare his glory among the nations"!

3) *A Chronological Structure.* The WCF course of study is based on a "time-frame sequence." This means that, instead of moving willy-nilly through course materials in accordance with whatever sequence or progression might be adopted by the professor, the structure of the entire course of WCF study is based upon the movement of history, especially upon history as "His story"—the large picture of what God is doing, past and present. To be more specific, the entire course of study is broken down into four modules:

First Module: First Things—Creation to 400 B.C.

Second Module: Formulation—400 B.C to A.D. 200

Third Module: Fruition—A.D. 200 to 1980

Fourth Module: Finalization—1980 to the Present

What is most important here is not the periodization as such, but rather the emphasis on the unfolding of God's plan from the beginning to the end of history as we know it.

4) *An Interdisciplinary Approach.* Fragmentation and nonintegration are avoided by refusing to "partition off" the various fields of study. The materials of the disciplines that go to make up a well-rounded education are studied in relationship to history. For example, the materials that go to make up a course in cultural anthropology are woven into the fabric of the four-module outline. So readings on the meaning of culture, distinctions between the cultural and the supracultural, and the development of separate cultures appear in relation to a study of the early chapters of Genesis. Kinship systems are con-

sidered in relation to a later study of the book of Ruth. And so on.

5) *A Student-Mentor Relationship.* In an arrangement reminiscent of that of pastoral studies in the early days of North American education, and also reflective of many doctoral programs currently, each WCF student works under the tutelage of a mentor. The mentor may be chosen by the student but, in any case, the mentor must qualify by meeting the requirements of the directors of the program. Mentoring is taken seriously by the directors. Mentors are provided with a wealth of information on program philosophy, course materials, the student-mentor relationship, and procedures. Students meet with their mentor on a weekly basis and for an extended period which is carefully structured.

6) *Extensive Course Materials.* Though students are expected to take full advantage of library resources available to them, the Institute for International Studies provides information on volumes to be acquired by the student, videotaped lectures, and manuals written and produced specially for the WCF course of study. Each component is important. Student purchases largely consist of the kind of reference works that will serve them well over a lifetime. Video lectures, for example, feature a complete series on Old Testament theology by Walter C. Kaiser and are augmented by his writings on the subject. (Since Kaiser takes a chronological approach to the study of Old Testament theology, both his methodology and materials fit hand-in-glove with the WCF program.) Manuals prepared specifically for students in the WCF program include detailed workbooks, integrated readings gathered from a wide variety of sources, and an illuminating mentor's handbook.

7) *A Detailed Schedule.* Unlike most correspondence degree programs, the WCF program is carefully designed to assure that students undertake a variety of learning activities, adhere to a regular schedule, accomplish specific goals, and complete the masters degree within a two-year period. The materials provided by the Institute both require and enable the

student to accomplish well-defined assignments on a daily and structured basis.

8) *Inductive Bible Study.* From the very beginning to the very end students are not only encouraged but also required, not only challenged but also instructed so to ensure that they will study the biblical text for themselves. For WCF students a concordance, preferably a concordance of the original language, takes precedence over a commentary. In fact, the commentaries are the last books to be consulted as students are led through the study process. First comes the larger context, then the particular passage at hand (the structure, the phraseology, the etymologies, the parallel passages), and, finally, the Bible commentaries and Bible handbooks.

9) *A Heuristic Philosophy.* Closely allied to the inductive method of Bible study is the deep-seated conviction that what a student discovers for herself or himself is much better remembered and used than what a student accepts from another. The words are a part of academic jargon but are used quite widely even in relation to Bible study so that it is important to distinguish between the two adjectives "heuristic" and "serendipitous." The latter refers more to chance discovery while the former has to do with demonstrating sound investigative methods. WCF students are taught to investigate for themselves and come up with defensible answers. But having done that, they are also taught to consider the works of those who have gone before. After all, the Bible is to be understood in the context of the church, not only or primarily in the closet or cloister.

10) *A Discipling Component.* Convinced that the best way to learn—really learn—any given body of material is to teach it to someone else, program planners have included assignments that require students to devise plans for teaching the various lessons. Moreover, they are expected to teach them to groups or at least share what they have learned with a friend, spouse or other family member.

Conclusion

It must have been something to be apprenticed to one or another of the great divines of eighteenth-century New England. But there was a lot those great men of God did not know, both of what had gone before and what has been discovered since. So it is that, in the providence of God, today's students are privileged to study with professors who have mastered anthropology, sociology, linguistics, communication, psychology and, especially, the languages, text and teachings of God's Word, the Bible.

Nevertheless, progress has been purchased at a price. Preparation today often extends over many years. Student families are relocated and must try to find new church homes and employment near the school. Budgets are strained to the breaking point. Studies are intense but fragmented. And graduates may still be unprepared to face the multi-cultured, multi-religious and still materialistic and morally bankrupt world of tomorrow. *The innovations of the WCF course of study are designed to resolve some of those problems by providing a new kind of integrated training for actual and potential church and mission leaders. Envision a situation where the motivated student studies under the tutelage of a mentor who is both a thinker and a practitioner, one who does not replace the experts but serves as a link to them. Where the primary textbook has been authored by the Living Lord of the universe, and all human productions and progress are measured by his revealed truth. Where studies are so arranged that geology and astronomy are studied concurrently with the Genesis account, and where the life and teachings of Confucius, Lao-tze, Gautama and Zoroaster are studied along with those of great Old Testament prophets like Isaiah, Jeremiah, Ezekiel and Daniel. Where it is but a step from the classroom to the mission field where people need to be confronted with the gospel and the sanctuary where believers need to be confirmed in the faith. Where learners become leaders by demonstrating faith, faithfulness and fruitfulness in the context of ministry.*

My purpose in writing this chapter is not to inspire some entrepreneur to go to Tokyo or Timbuktu and start the "Christian School of the Future." Nor is it my special purpose to promote the World Christian Foundations curriculum as such, even though I am not aware of any other curriculum on planet earth that incorporates and integrates such a massive amount of relevant knowledge into a framework that is so thoroughly and unapologetically biblical. Rather, my purpose is to encourage all who have important roles in selecting and training the Christian leaders of today and tomorrow to take another look at what is happening and what should be happening. In almost any given situation we can work to preserve the gains and plug the gaps observable in current programs and contemporary practice. In making that attempt, we would do well to review the World Christian Foundation program and philosophy. WCF makes integrated training available to leaders in the field and leaders "in process." *Adopt and adapt, but of two things we can rest assured. One: the only hope left to a postmodern world is that it hear, believe and obey the Divine Word. Two: the best training that church and mission can possibly provide is one that prepares leaders to understand and proclaim that Word. All of it.*

Part IV

Conclusion

11

Forward to the Future

We began this book by suggesting that Christians need to keep an eye on the past in order to have a proper perspective on the present and the future. Now as we come to the end of the book, it would seem appropriate to consider the words of the apostle Paul when he writes:

> but this one thing I do: forgetting what lies behind and reaching forward to what lies ahead, I press on toward the goal for the prize of the upward call of God in Christ Jesus. Let us therefore, as many as are perfect, have this attitude; and if in anything you have a different attitude, God will reveal that also to you (Phil. 3:13b-15).

Indeed, those are appropriate words with which to end this book. And we will consider them. But first we remind ourselves once again that, though some things are to be forgotten as soon as possible, other things are to be remembered forever. In great measure, successful Christian living and serving depends upon remembering that which should be remembered and forgetting that which should be forgotten. That distinction is the focus of these final paragraphs.

The "So Thats" and "Now Therefores" of Three Missionary Passages in the Old Testament

It has been common in church and mission circles to think of Israel's mission in the Old Testament as "come-structured" and the church's mission in the New Testament as "go-structured." Israel's role in Old Testament times is widely believed to have been a passive one—they were just to *be there* as the "people of God" so that representatives of other nations could come to Israel and learn about the true God. The church's role in this New Testament era, on the other hand, is held to be an active one. The church is *sent* with the gospel. The church is to go and share the truth of God with all the peoples of the earth.

One who takes issue with that understanding as it relates to the Old Testament is Walter C. Kaiser, Jr. He insists that Israel's role was meant to be an active one—Israel was *sent* to the nations. In support of this thesis, he cites Old Testament history and, especially, three basic passages: Genesis 12:1-3, Exodus 19:4-6, and Psalm 67 (Kaiser 1992: A-26-33).

In the familiar promise to Abraham in Genesis 12, God promised blessing after blessing upon him and his descendants. But that is not all. Kaiser notes a shift in verb tense and says that a purpose clause should be included when translating the passage. Speaking to Abraham, God promised to blessed him, make his name great and make of him a great nation "*so that* in you all the families of earth might be blessed" (Kaiser 1992: A-27; emphasis his).

Similarly, in the famous "Eagle's Wings Speech" in Exodus 19, God reminded the Israelites that he miraculously brought them out of Egypt and to himself for a purpose. His word was, *"Now therefore"* and then he went on to tell them that if they would obey his voice and keep his covenant they would be his special possession [moveable treasure], a kingdom of priests [royal priests], and a holy nation [wholly the Lord's nation] (Kaiser 1992: A-29-30; emphasis his).

Again, in Psalm 67 the Psalmist built upon the Aaronic benediction (Num. 6:24-26) but he substituted Elohim (God's name used in relationship to all humanity) for Yahweh (his covenantal name in relationship to Israel) and he also changed "upon us" to "among us." So the graciousness, blessing and shining face of God was not for Israel's sake alone. God had a purpose in mind: *"so that* your way may be known upon the earth, your salvation among all nations (or Gentiles)" (Kaiser 1994: A-31; emphasis mine).

Kaiser's point, then, is that God's promises to Israel must be understood in the light of his plan and purpose to make himself and his ways known to the nations. His promise, purpose, plan, proclamation, plea—all have to do with Israel's mission to the world. When Abraham's sons and daughters "forgot to remember" God's purpose and sold their brother into slavery, God took them all into Egypt and through the faithfulness of Joseph and Moses demonstrated his person and power. When they became chauvinistic he nevertheless caused Nineveh to repent through the proclamation of a reluctant Jonah. When they proved incorrigible, he allowed their defeat and deportation to Babylon where Daniel and his friends refused to bow down to Nebuchadnezzar's image and bore witness to the God of heaven. When Israel hoarded and even distorted his Word, God made possible a Greek translation (the Septuagint) which became the Bible of most of the New Testament authors and the most potent weapon wielded by the early church in its missionary outreach.

Of course, the greatest failure of all was Israel's rejection of their Messiah. But God turned even that colossal failure into the fulfillment of his purpose. He raised up a "people who were not a people" to be his moveable treasure, his royal priesthood, his holy nation (1 Pet. 2:9-10). That brings us to the New Testament church and its mission.

The "Wherefores" and "Therefores" of Three New Testament Passages

If there is any doubt at all about Israel's mission in Old Testament times, there should be no doubt whatsoever about the mission of the church in the New Testament. Nevertheless, as we have noted previously, the church has not always recognized its mission in the past and there are indications that it may be in process of forgetting or mistaking it today. A very recent poll conducted by the Institute for Research in Social Science at the University of North Carolina indicates that the Great Commission is not taken all that seriously by American Christians today. When asked to rank the various roles of the church in order of their importance, only thirty-two percent of American Christians considered converting others to the faith as a "very important" activity of the church. Even among the usually more conservative Christians of the South only slightly more than half (fifty-two percent) ranked it as very important. It was outranked by providing moral guidance for young people (ninety-one percent), making worship opportunities (eighty-seven percent) and helping the needy (eighty-six percent) (*Christian Century* Vol.. 111 No. 19, p. 601).

Lest we, like Israel, forget what our mission really is, we will look at three New Testament passages before concluding this book. All three are characterized by the use of two small three-letter words (in the Greek) that are translated as "wherefore" and "therefore" and require us to look back before moving ahead.

First, at the risk of redundancy, we note the words of the Great Commission in Matthew 28:16-20 yet once more. We did not emphasize it previously, but it should be noted now that the force of Jesus' command rests squarely on the fact that all authority in heaven and earth has been committed to him. For the church, world mission is a simple matter of obedience. But it is more than that, so let us move on.

Second, we come to the apostle Paul's familiar exhortation in Romans 12:1: "I urge you therefore, . . . that you present your bodies a living and holy sacrifice . . . which is your spiritual service of worship." This particular "therefore" takes us back to a rather extended argument. In a nutshell the argument is as follows.

In Romans 1 through 8 Paul has systematically taken his readers from the doctrines of sin and lostness to santification and glorification. Then he imagines his readers saying something like, "That's great, Paul. But if God can forget Plan A (Israel) and go to Plan B (the church), what is to prevent him from forgetting Plan B and going to Plan C, whatever that might be?"

Paul's response is unequivocal. God has not been taken by surprise. There is only one plan. Abraham's descendants include all people of true faith (chapter 9); the gospel is to be preached to all and "whosoever will" can be saved (chapter 10); and, oh yes, when the "fulness of the Gentiles" has come in, God is going to deal with Israel as a nation again and save them (chapter 11:1-29). The bottom line is this: God shuts up all in disobedience so he can show mercy to all. No one would have known this apart from revelation. No one "advised" God. No one had this mercy coming as his or her "just deserts." Everything is from God, through God and to God. To him be the glory forever. So be it (chapter 11:30-36).

Therefore, Paul writes, present your bodies as a living sacrifice, refuse to conform to the age, renew your mind, and you will find out by experience that which is good, acceptable and perfect—the will of God (chapter 12:1, 2). *The first of the "Four Spiritual Laws" (God loves you and has a wonderful plan for your life) is indeed true. At least, it is true for the believer. But it is not "first." First comes the fact that God has a wonderful plan, period. Study THAT plan. Learn THAT plan.*

Master THAT plan. Revel in THAT plan. Give yourself to THAT plan. THEN you will discover that, as a part of THAT plan, God has a wonderful plan for your life as well!

Third, there is one more "wherefore, therefore" passage that we should not overlook. It is in 2 Peter 3 where the apostle Peter writes about people in the last days who will say that history just repeats itself and will scoff at the idea of Christ's return. They "deliberately forget" (NIV) about nonrepeatable divine action in creating the world and sending the flood (3:5-7). Believers should not forget, however. Nor should we forget that he is coming; that he wants as many as possible to be saved; that the earth will be destroyed in a gigantic conflagration; that there will be a new heaven and earth of righteousness; and that we should be looking for and hastening his coming (3:8-13).

Wherefore, says Peter, we should be diligent to be found in him and regard his patience as a salvation opportunity. *Therefore,* he says, we should be on guard against error and be growing in grace (3:14-18). That which is deliberately forgotten by scoffers leads to their destruction. That which is dutifully remembered by saints leads to their salvation *and* the salvation of others!

Facing the Future

Finally, then, we return to that intriguing passage in Philippians where Paul's testimony is that, "forgetting what lies behind" and "reaching forward to what lies ahead," he presses on "toward the goal for the prize of the upward call of God in Christ Jesus" (3:13-14).

In context, Paul first speaks of his *salvation*—of the fact that, if righteousness is attained by works, status or zeal, he has an inside track (3:4-6). But righteousness comes by faith in Christ, so he has put all of those supposed advantages on the debit side of the ledger (3:7). He then speaks of his *service*—the fact that, as an "apostle-missionary," he has given up everything and counted it loss in order to "gain Christ" and "attain to the resurrection from the dead" (3:8-11). Now in prison Paul is prepared to forget about those sacrifices and face the future. Two aspects of his "attitude" or perspective are especially germane.

First, there is the negative "forgetting" aspect. But forgetting must be the right kind. In the biblical sense "forgetting" is not so much blotting out of memory. That may be impossible. It is more a refusal to allow the past to influence present or future attitudes and actions. It is the opposite of the biblical "remembering" we considered in the first chapter of this book—the remembering that involves recalling the past in such a way as to make the past a potent part of present and future attitudes and conduct (Martin 1959: 153). Note also that "forgetting" here is a present participle, indicating that Paul deliberately and continuously refused to let his past prerogatives as a Jew, or his sacrifices as an apostle of Christ, influence the present or future.

Second, there is a positive "reaching" aspect of Paul's attitude. His immediate prospects were clouded with uncertainty. But beyond that immediate and uncertain future, there was a prize—a high or "upward call of Christ Jesus" (3:14). Paul looked *ahead,* but he also looked *beyond* to the time of his meeting with the Lord himself. He kept his eye on that meeting; he "reached" for it much as a runner "reaches" out for the finish line. The imagery here in Philippians is much the same as Paul had used earlier when writing to the Corinthians. There he noted that, while many run in any given race, only one receives the prize. Then he testified that he was running with the prize in view; that he kept his body in submission lest, after preaching to others, he himself be disqualified (1 Cor. 9:24-27).

Is not Paul's testimony most appropriate as we bring our considerations here to a close? As Christ's representatives in the world, we do take with us our racial identity and citizenship, our education or lack of it, and our status whether high or low. All of that means nothing when it comes to salvation. But it does mean something when it comes to strategizing and service. We know that. And the fact that Paul knew it becomes apparent when you follow him in his preaching and teaching ministry throughout the first century Mediterranean world. Repeatedly we find him capitalizing on his birth, his Roman citizenship, and his educational and religious background. But while he capitalized on these things but he did not consider them to be crucial. What was crucial was that which he had received by "revelation through Jesus Christ" (Gal. 1:12).

And so it will be with us and our progeny as we look ahead to our service in the postmodern world. Who we are, where we come from, what we have learned and how we apply it—all of this will make a difference. But it will not make the crucial difference. *Looking ahead,* what will matter most in our postmodern world will have to do with divine revelation—with how it is delivered and how it is received.

But that is not the end of the matter either. Paul understood that there is still more to this matter of Christian service. It has to do with the point at which conservative evangelicalism has proved itself to be most vulnerable in modern times. *Looking beyond* the postmodern world to his coming, we may expect some approbation for our efforts to defend and disseminate God's Word. But while it is one thing to agree to Scripture authority, it is another thing to live under that authority. It is one thing to interpret the Bible with a runaway world in view, but it is another thing to interpret it with our own wayward tendencies in view. It is one thing to apply God's Word to the world, but that is not the same as applying it to ourselves and the church. Perhaps the greatest obstacle to an evangelized world today was reflected in the statement of the Ceylonese Buddhist professor who said, "I think you Christians are very ordinary people who, nevertheless, make very extraordinary claims."

Thinking, then, in terms of our own judgment, what will matter most as we enter the kingdom will not be so much whether or not we have run, but whether or not we have run so as to receive the prize. What will matter will not be simply a matter of whether or not we have preached to others, but whether we have preached to ourselves.

Bibliography

Allen, Roland
1962 *The Spontaneous Expansion of the Church.* Grand Rapids: Wm. B. Eerdmans Publishing Co.

Almy, Gary, and Carol Tharp Almy, with Jerry Jenkins
1994 *Addicted to Recovery.* Eugene, OR: Harvest House Publishers.

Archer, Gleason
1982 *An Encyclopedia of Bible Difficulties.* Chicago: Moody Press.

Augsburger, David W.
1984 *Pastoral Counseling Across Cultures.* Philadelphia: The Westminster Press.

Barney, G. Linwood
1976 "The Supracultural and the Cultural: Implications for Frontier Missions." In R. Pierce Beaver, ed. *The Gospel and Frontier Peoples: A Report of a Consultation December 1972*, pp. 48-57. Pasadena: William Carey Library.

Bruce, F. F.
  1953 "Foreword." In *The Dawn of World Redemption: A Survey of Historical Revelation in the Old Testament.* Erich Sauer; G. H. Lang, trans., p. 7. Carlisle, United Kingdom: The Paternoster Press, Ltd.

Carson, Donald A.
  1979 "Response." In *New Horizons in World Mission: Evangelicals and the Christian Mission in the 1980s.* David J. Hesselgrave, ed. pp. 228-32. Grand Rapids: Baker Book House.

Christianity Today
  1981 "The Concerns and Considerations of Carl F. H. Henry." 25, no. 5 (March): 18-23.

Christianity Today
  1994 "Converting Others Not a High Priority." 3, no. 19 (June 15-22): 601.

Chirgwin, A. M.
  1954 *The Bible in World Evangelism.* London: SCM Press Ltd.

Collins, Gary, ed.
  1980 *Helping People Grow: Practical Approaches to Christian Counseling.* Santa Ana: Vision House.

Crabb, Larry
  1993 *Finding God.* Grand Rapids: Zondervan Publishing House.

D'Aubigne, J. H. M.
  1840 *History of the Great Reformation,* 3rd ed. London: D. Walther.

Davis, John Jefferson, ed.
1978   *The Necessity of Systematic Theology.* 2nd ed. Grand Rapids: Baker Book House.

Donovan, Vincent J.
1978   *Christianity Rediscovered.* Chicago: Fides/Claretian Press.

Dyrness, William A.
1990   *Learning About Theology From The Third World.* Grand Rapids: Zondervan Publishing House.

Engel, James F.
1990   "We are the World." *Christianity Today* 34, no. 13 (September 24): 32-34.

Fleming, Bruce C. E.
1980   *Contextualization of Theology: An Evangelical Assessment.* Pasadena: William Carey Library.

Fosdick, Harry Emerson.
1924   *The Modern Use of the Bible.* New York: Macmillan Press.

Gerstner, John H.
1965   *Theology for Everyman.* Chicago: Moody Press.

Griffiths, Michael
1967   *You and God's Work Overseas.* Chicago: InterVarsity Press.

Gutierrez, Gustavo.
1973   *A Theology of Liberation.* Caridad Inda and John Eagleson, trans. and ed. New York: Orbis Publishing Co.

Henry, Carl F. H.
1976-83 *God, Revelation and Authority*, 6 vols. Waco: Word Books.

1979   "The Authority and Inspiration of the Bible." In *The Expositor's Bible Commentary,* Vol 1. Frank E. Gaebelein, gen. ed., pp. 3-35. Grand Rapids: Zondervan Publishing House.

Hesselgrave, David J.
1984   *Counseling Cross-Culturally: An Introduction to Theory and Practice for Christians.* Grand Rapids: Baker Book House.

1988   *Today's Choices for Tomorrow's Mission: An Evangelical Perspective On Trends and Issues in Missions.* Grand Rapids: Zondervan Publishing House.

1991   *Communicating Christ Cross-Culturally: An Introduction to Missionary Communication*, rev. ed. Grand Rapids: Zondervan Publishing House.

Hesselgrave, David J. and Edward Rommen
1989   *Contextualization: Meanings, Methods and Models.* Grand Rapids: Baker Book House.

Hiebert, Paul. G.
1982   "The Flaw of the Excluded Middle." *Missiology* 10 (January): 35-47.

1987   "Critical Contextualization." *Missology* 12 (July): 287-96. Reprinted in *Notes in Anthropology and Intercultural Community Work* 12 (December): 5-23. Reprinted in *The Best in Theology: Vol. Two*, J. I. Packer, gen. ed. Carol Stream: Christianity Today, Inc., n.d. Revised and reprinted in *The International Bulletin of Missionary Research* 11, no. 3: 104-12.

1989   "Form and Meaning in the Contextualization of the Gospel." In *The Word Among Us*, Dean S. Gilliland, ed., pp. 101-120. Dallas: Word Publishing.

1994   "Form and Meaning in Contextualization." Paper given at a Midwest regional meeting of the Evangelical Missiological Society and the Evangelical Theological Society in Wheaton, Illinois, March 18, 1994.

Hunter, James
1983   *Evangelicalism: Conservative Religion and the Quandry of Modernity.* New Brunswick, NJ: Rutgers University Press.

1987   *Evangelicalism: The Coming Generation.* Chicago: University of Chicago Press.

International Review of Mission
1981   "The Bible in Mission." 70, no. 279 (July): entire issue.

Johnson, Elliott E.
1990   *Expository Hermeneutics: An Introduction.* Grand Rapids: Zondervan Publishing House.

Johnston, A. P.
1974   *World Evangelism and the Word of God.* Minneapolis: Bethany.

1983   "The Use of the Bible in World Evangelization." In *The Living and Active Word of God: Studies in Honor of Samuel J. Schultz.* Morris Inch and Ronald Youngblood, eds., pp. 309-320. Winona Lake, IN: Eisenraunf.

Kaiser, Walter C., Jr.
1978   *Toward an Old Testament Theology.* Grand Rapids: Zondervan Publishing House.

1992   "Israel's Missionary Call." In *Perspectives on the World Christian Movement: A Reader*, rev. ed. Ralph D. Winter and Steven C. Hawthorne, gen. eds. pp. A25-A33. Pasadena: William Carey Library.

Kayser, John G.
1992   "The Effect of Field Problems and Stressors on Missionary Attrition." Paper delivered at the annual conference of the Evangelical Missiological Society (Canada Region) and the Association of Canadian Bible Colleges at Three Hills, Alberta, May 12-13.

Kenney, Jim
1993   *1993: The Parliament of the World's Religions.* Chicago: The Council for a Parliament of the World's Religions.

Klein, William W., Craig L. Blomberg, and Robert L. Hubbard, Jr.
1993   *Introduction to Biblical Interpretation.* Kermit A. Ecklebarger, consulting ed. Dallas: Word.

Larkin, William J., Jr.
1993   *Culture and Biblical Hermeneutics: Interpreting and Applying the Authoritative Word in a Relatavistic Age.* Lanham, New York, London: University Press of America.

Lapsley, James N.
1969   "Pastoral Theology Past and Present." In *The New Shape of Pastoral Theology: Essays in Honor of Seward Hiltner*, edited by William B. Oglesby, Jr.,

pp. 31-48. Nashville: Abingdon Press.

Martin, Ralph P.
1959   *The Epistle of Paul to the Philippians: An Introduction and Commentary. The Tyndale New Testament Commentaries,* R. V. G. Tasker, gen. ed. Grand
Rapids: Wm. B. Eerdmans Publishing Co.

McIlwain, Trevor
1981   *Notes on the Chronological Approach to Evangelism
and Church Planting.* Sanford, FL: New Tribes Mission.

1987   *Building on Firm Foundations,* Vol. 1, *Guidelines for
Evangelism and Teaching Believers.* Sanford, FL:
New Tribes Mission.

1988a   *Building on Firm Foundations,* Vol. 2, *Evangelism:
The Old Testament.* Sanford, FL: New Tribes Mission.

1988b   *Building on Firm Foundations,* Vol. 3, *Evangelism:
The Life of Christ.* Sanford, FL: New Tribes Mission.

McIlwain, Trevor with Nancy Everson
1991   *Firm Foundations: Creation to Christ.* Sanford, FL:
New Tribes Mission.

Mickelsen, A. Berkley
1963   *Interpreting the Bible.* Grand Rapids: Wm. B. Eerdmans Publishing Co.

Newbigin, Lesslie
1987   *Mission in Christ's Way: Bible Studies.* Geneva:
WCC Publications.

1989   *The Gospel in a Pluralist Society.* Grand Rapids: Wm. B. Eerdmans Publishing Co..

1991   *Truth to Tell: The Gospel as Public Truth.* Grand Rapids: Wm. B. Eerdmans Publishing Co.

Nicholls, Bruce J.
1979   *Contextualization: A Theology of Gospel and Culture.* Downers Grove, IL: InterVarsity Press.

Osborne, Grant R.
1991   *The Hermeneutical Spiral: A Comprehensive Introduction to Biblical Interpretation.* Downers Grove: InterVarsity Press.

Osborne, William L.
1993   "Genesis 12-50." In *Foundations of Global Civilization: Semester One, covering the time frame from Creation to 400 B.C.,* Mentors Handbook, 18:1-6. Pasadena: Institute of International Studies, U.S. Center for World Mission.

Piper, John
1990   *The Supremacy of God in Preaching.* Grand Rapids: Baker Book House.

1991   *The Pleasures of God.* Portland: Multnomah Press.

1993   *Let the Nations Be Glad!: The Supremacy of God in Missions.* Grand Rapids: Baker Book House.

Rommen, Edward
1994   "The Detheologization of Missiology." In *The Trinity World Forum*, Winter, 1994.

Sauer, Erich
1952a *Revelation in the New Testament.* G. H. Lang, trans. Grand Rapids: Wm. B. Eerdmans Publishing Co.

1952b *The Triumph of the Crucified: A Survey of Historical Revelation in the New Testament.* G. H. Lang, trans. Grand Rapids: Wm. B. Eerdmans Publishing Co.

1953 *The Dawn of World Redemption: A Survey of Historical Revelation in the Old Testament.* G. H. Lang, trans. Carlisle, the United Kingdom: The Paternoster Press, Ltd.

1954 *From Eternity to Eternity: An Outline of the Divine Purposes.* G. H. Lang, trans. Grand Rapids: Wm. B. Eerdmans Publishing Co.

Scherer, James A.
1987 *Gospel, Church, and Kingdom: Comparative Studies in World Mission Theology.* Minneapolis: Augsburg Publishing House.

Schrenk, Gottlob
1964 In *Theological Dictionary of the New Testament.* Vol. 2, Geoffrey W. Bromiley, ed. and trans. pp. 93-98. Grand Rapids: Wm. B. Eerdmans Publishing Co.

Sharpe, Eric J.
1971 *Fifty Key Words: Comparative Religion.* Richmond: John Knox Press.

1974 "The Goals of Inter-Religious Dialogue." In *Truth and Dialogue in World Religions: Conflicting Truth-Claims.* John Hick, ed. Philadelphia: Westminister Press.

Stott, John R. W.
  1975   *Christian Mission in the Modern World*. London: Falcon Press.
  1992   "The Bible in World Evangelization." In *Perspectives on the World Christian Movement*, rev. ed. Ralph D. Winter and Steven C. Hawthorne, gen. eds., pp. A3-A9. Pasadena: The William Carey Library.

Stott, John R. W. and Coote, Robert T., eds.
  1979   *Gospel and Culture*. Pasadena: William Carey Library.

  1980   *Down to Earth: Studies in Christianity and Culture*. Grand Rapids: Wm. B. Eerdmans Publishing Co.

Thiselton, Anthony C.
  1977   "New Hermeneutic." In *N.T. Interpretation: Essays on Principles and Methods*. I. Howard Marshall. ed. pp. 75-104. Grand Rapids: Wm. B. Eerdmans Publishing Co.

  1980   *The Two Horizons: New Testament Hermeneutics and Philosophical Description with Special Reference to Heidegger, Bultmann, Gadamer, and Wittgenstein*. Grand Rapids: Wm. B. Eerdmans Publishing Co.

Veith, G. Edward, Jr.
  1994   *Postmodern Times*. Wheaton: Crossway Books.

Voss, Geerhardus
  1948   *Biblical Theology: Old and New Testaments*. Grand Rapids: Wm. B. Eerdmans Publishing Co.

Warfield, B. B.
  1978   "The Idea of Systematic Theology." In *The Necessity of Systematic Theology*, second ed. John Jefferson

Davis, ed. pp. 127-68. Grand Rapids: Wm. B. Eerdmans Publishing Co.

Warner, Timothy M.
1991   *Spiritual Warfare.* Wheaton: Crossway Books.

n.d.   *A Manual for Resolving Spiritual Conflicts in Cross-Cultural Ministries,* mimeographed.

Weber, Hans-Ruedi
1957   *The Communication of the Gospel to Illiterates: Based on a Missionary Experience in Indonesia.* London: SCM Press.

1981   *Experiments With Bible Study.* Geneva: WCC Publications.

1989   *Power: Focus for a Biblical Theology.* Geneva: WCC Publications.

Wells, David F.
1990   "Word and World: Biblical Authority and the Quandry of Modernity." In *Evangelical Affirmations.* Kenneth S. Kantzer and Carl F.H. Henry, eds. pp. 153-77. Grand Rapids: Zondervan Publishing House.

1992   *No Place for Truth: Or, Whatever Happened to Evangelical Theology?* Grand Rapids: Wm. B. Eerdmans Publishing Co.

Winter, Ralph D.
1993   "The Theology of the Law of God." In *Foundations of Global Civilization: Semester One.* Mentors Handbook. pp. 27:1-10. Pasadena: Institute of International Studies, U.S. Center for World Mision.

1994   "Radical Breakthrough: Combatting the 2nd Largest Obstacle in Missions." In *Mission Frontiers Bulletin*, March-April: 3.

Winter, Ralph D. and Steven Hawthorne, eds.
1981   *Perspectives on the World Christian Movement.* Pasadena: William Carey Library.

World Pulse
1993   Vol. 28, no. 5 (Feb. 12):

Wright, G. Ernest
1991   "Biblical Theology (OT). Introduction." In *New 20th Century Encyclopedia of Religious Knowledge.* J. D. Douglas, ed. pp. 101-104. Grand Rapids: Baker Book House.

Yoder, Perry B.
1978   *Toward an Understanding of the Bible.* Newton, KS: Faith and Life.